T0152695

FROM CRISIS TO
COMMUNISATION

Revolutionary Pocketbooks

FROM CRISIS TO COMMUNISATION

Gilles Dauvé

From Crisis to Communisation
Gilles Dauvé
This edition copyright © 2019 PM Press
All rights reserved. No part of this book may be transmitted by any
means without permission in writing from the publisher.

ISBN: 9781629630991
Library of Congress Control Number: 2015930885

Cover by John Yates/Stealworks
Layout by Jonathan Rowland based on work by briandesign

10 9 8 7 6 5 4 3 2 1

PM Press
PO Box 23912
Oakland, CA 94623
www.pmpress.org

■ CONTENTS

■ COMMUNISATION AND MY DISCONTENT

"For several years now, the theme of communisation has led to controversies that are very often ill-informed," Bruno Astarian wrote in 2010.[1]

An understatement. In recent years, *communisation* has become one of the radical in-words, whose popularity extends far beyond the regrettably called "communisers." In a transatlantic game of Chinese whispers, the notion has developed into an elasticity of meaning and is now a blanket term covering a wide range of attitudes and theories.[2] The differences among these are both substantial and consequential.[3]

A truly valid and stimulating approach to revolution is mixed with a deceptive reconstruction of history that divides it into two completely different phases and presents a catastrophe-happy view of the present, akin to a final crisis theory, though nobody expresses it in such plain words.

Many communisation theorists behave as if they had found the solution once and for all and present our time as a period when the proletarian movement has and can only have one goal: communism.

In spite of its extremist outlook, is it all that different from what could be heard in 1970? In the bygone days of workerist Leninist party-building and counterculture experimenting, a lot of radicals also believed their version of revolution meant changing everything: We want the world and we want it now! Forty years later, *communisation* serves as a convenient reference point, like Marxism (or, for others, anarchism) to which a very heterogeneous set of ideas can be added: it provides people with a supposedly solid and undisputed common ground on which they feel free to combine class, gender, race, alternative art, and perhaps ecology. If capitalism is about to die, everything is permitted.

Here is our basic disagreement with a lot of "communisers": They regard communisation as the long-wanted and at-last-found answer to the revolutionary question, and consequently regard themselves as providers of this ultimate answer.

There is no privileged vantage point where the meaning of all history is revealed, and one of the main points this book will make is that the idea of communisation was and remains a product of its time. The communisation concept depends upon a specific period, a specific crisis, and the other major crisis we are now going through has bearing on its evolution.

This is neither a history of ideas nor an impersonal story. We will have to recall where a number of comrades came from and what they did in the late 1960s, what part they played around 1968 and how they understood it, went back to Marx, to the German-Dutch and Italian Lefts, and read the Situationists, how the notion of communisation emerged and what has become of it since.

CHAPTER 1

■ LEGACY

§ 1: Back to the 1960s–70s

Let's start with a hard fact: in the 1960s and '70s, the proletarians did not cross the Rubicon.

Fordism had reached its zenith at the same time as it intensified work and as dissatisfaction about consumer society started to grow. That double cause resulted in the combination of worker unrest and a critique of daily life, which launched a long proletarian wave.

When the movement lost its critical edge, its manifold aspects turned into fragmented piecemeal transformations. The workplace became the scene of a neo-unionism, albeit with little new union creation. Armed violence disconnected itself from social disturbances. Women's action withdrew into feminism. The critique of the party led to the launching of grouplets, and the critique of vanguardism ended in rank-and-filism. Rebellious marginality got integrated into acceptable street culture. The critique of daily life gave birth to alternativism and cyberindividualism. Instead of anti-imperialist and anti-military actions, the 2003 Iraq War coincided with the heyday of consensual pacifism.

This was no novelty: revolutionary failures unleash reaction and recuperation.

The big turn lay elsewhere: no radical grassroots organisation was born out of this worldwide storm, even in countries which were at the peak of the movement, and those organisations that emerged were short-lived, or merged with former organisations, unions usually. The Argentine *Cordobazo* popular uprising of 1969 did not create large sustainable organisations, and neither did the widespread worker insubordination and street rioting in the mid-1970s in Italy. New bodies or break-away unions spring up all the time, with little foothold in the working class.

This major change went rather unnoticed at the time and still is.

All previous unrest or insurrectionary periods had resulted in the creation of new forms, whether party, union, or autonomous body. In the West and in Japan, since the demise of the Spanish Workers' Party of Marxist Unification (POUM) in 1937, no far-left party with strongholds in the workplace has been founded and has managed to fight on. Nothing comparable to early twentieth-century social democracy, Stalinist parties, or the 1930s CIO. Syriza is just about capable of moderating unrest in Greece: it proves incapable of putting forth a platform alternative to mainstream bourgeois politics.

One of the main reasons for this is the lack of *intermediate* demands capable of gathering mass support in the working class, as universal suffrage, the eight-hour day, union rights, labour laws, and paid holidays had done before World War II. Whatever the causes, this meant the real end of the worker movement as we had known it. Its later decline, under the combined pressures of unemployment, deindustrialisation and repression, as exemplified by the English miners' defeat in 1984–85, was a dramatic yet secondary matter.

The absence of any serious attempt to create new, permanent grassroots organisations is all the more striking considering that one of the main features of the period was the persistent effort to achieve *autonomy*. Though party and union bureaucrats were still able to mediate between labour and capital, they came under criticism and sometimes attack as they had not been since the German *Unionen* after 1918. Only a minority rejected bureaucracy, institutions, and authority, but it was a militant minority, usually the initiators of strikes and riots, and not just in Western Europe or the United States.

Unlike post-1917, there was no attempt to seize political power or to take over the workplace. Factory occupation was the bother of a fraction of the labour force, often the union activists, and in Italy quite a few occupiers preferred to sleep at home.

Politically, nobody expected a truly different policy from a socialist or popular government if it came to power. Since then, the traditional platform of the left (to make the poor richer, and the potent less powerful) has lost credibility and at best is seen as the least-bad option on offer. The communist parties have gone social democrat and the leftists look like what the CPs used to be—minus Stalinism.

Traditional solutions seemed outmoded. Cooperation and self-management were and are only implemented when the bosses leave, seen for example on a large scale in Portugal in 1974–75 and on a smaller scale in Argentina after 2001.

On the other hand, while the "old" worker movement has not given itself new forms, there are no radical programmes either: nothing like the 1919 German *Unionen*, no worker councils with the prospect of taking over and managing production.

Then and now, grassroots activity is local and basis-centred. Party-builders are derided: Lenin's democratic centralism is out, autonomy is the "in thing." Ex-Trots claim to be bottom-up. *Call* has more readers than *What Is to Be Done?* No more parties: this is the age of associations, info kiosks, networks, NGOs . . .

Meanwhile, the bourgeois hold the fort and are strong enough to make people believe that there is no such thing as a bourgeoisie anymore, that the big social divide is no longer between classes, only between rich and poor—a gap that can be bridged by a slow trickle-down process (liberal option), or by a fair sharing of riches (reformist option). Parliamentary democracy is mocked but still finds the means to fill in the political vacuum.[1] As is plain to see, no far-reaching reform is on the way and nowhere is society on the verge of any kind of revolution.

In sum, radical critique is left with more negative than positive certainties.[2]

§ 2: Three Steps to Capitalist Dominion

Step One was the containment and repression of the 1960s and '70s upsurge in the street and the workplace.

Without this, there would have been no Step Two: the re-imposition of work and reshuffling of capital, or in economists' terms business reengineering.

Step Three complemented One and Two by a flourish of theories according to which work was becoming inessential and the capital/labour relation no longer central. Class (and class struggle) had ceased to be a basic concept. If there was to be social change, it would not oppose the working class to a ruling bourgeoisie, but a shoreless popular whole to an anonymous shapeless domination. As in ballroom dancing, all three steps were concomitant: the popularity of the supposedly new social critique was and remains a by-product of the double process of proletarian defeat plus capitalist reorganisation.

To understand how capitalism regained the upper hand forty years ago, and has managed to keep it since, partial explanations are not enough:

The worker *bureaucracy*, this century-old enemy of radicalism, contained the surge because the proletarians allowed it. However infuriating this sounds to believers in worker pure class identity, union and party leadership only stifles proletarian autonomy when the rank and file limits itself to collective bargaining, even with militant and sometimes violent means.

Protest and unrest were not drowned in the flow of *consumerism*. True, contemporary individual objects (from the personal computer of the 1980s to current smartphone) have "recuperated" the demand for freedom typical of the 1960s and '70s . But consumer habits were in full bloom when the radical tide of that period happened, so they are not enough to prevent social unrest. Presenting consumption as a determinant is mistaking an effect for a cause. Capitalism is not run by supermarket shopping but by production for value and value accumulation. Indeed, a sign of capitalist victory is its ability to picture itself as a "consumer society." (A side effect is the description of *over*-consumption as responsible for ecological disasters present and future, implying that the culprit is none other than you and me.)[3]

Modern capitalist is no "abstainer," and even labour is invited to buy. But mass consumption is always ruled by the "iron law" of accumulation, and the affluent society has poverty in its midst. About 15 percent of the German population live below the poverty threshold (60 percent of the average net income) in the "richest" European country.

Volumes have being written about the shift from a managerial to a *shareholder capitalism*. However true that is, managers and shareholders alike are driven by cost-benefit ratio, return on investment, viz. profitability. Managers came to the fore in the first half of the twentieth century when private ownership proved inadequate to promote business and deal with organised labour. And in the last decades of the century, shareholder power asserted itself only *after* worker insubordination had been squelched.

Equally misleading is the explanation of the working debacle by *foreign cost-cutting competition*. This is forgetting that Mexican, Philippine, Chinese, and Romanian businessmen did not force their way into North American, Japanese, and West European markets. Outsourcing was initiated by the then-dominant national bourgeoisies *after* they had checked labour rebellion. Nowadays most of downsizing in the old industrial metropolises is due not to goods being manufactured in Asia but to productivity rises in Western and Japanese factories which need less labour to produce more.

Another fashionable school of thought insists on the *new spirit of capitalism*, which is said to have traded the hierarchical Fordist structure for a network-based organisation founded on team management, employee initiative and work autonomy.[4] With a condescending look down upon blue-collar workers unable to see beyond their machine tools and assembly lines, sociologists explain how crafty bosses recuperated the 1968 "artistic critique" of alienation and authority. The twenty-first century factory would be a place where labour is controlled by appealing to creativity, mobility, training, multitasking, and individual self-empowerment.

This is valid as long as one forgets the difference between management textbooks and life on the shop floor, between ideology and reality. The modern factory is authoritarian, and neo-Taylorism dominates the emerging countries. But above all and once again, law and order had first to be reintroduced in the workplace and in the street before new management techniques could be introduced and forced upon labour.

A deeper interpretation stressed the *interiorisation of capital*. The '68 rebels wanted to be free but, as they did not question capitalism, they were granted capitalist freedom. Since the failure of (bureaucratic) socialism with a human face, we would now live as humans with a capitalist face and mind: what Jacques Camatte called the *anthropomorphosis of capital*, which allegedly succeeds in remodelling us and creating a permanent addictive behaviour, where hyperactivity is in fact a passive compulsion to buy and consume.[5] This vision has the merit of emphasising how capitalism feeds on human reality: capitalism is a vampire . . . that perpetuates its victims. But that illustrates a weakness as much as its triumph. What is most striking is rather capital's *inability* to take any shape and form: such a plastic system *cannot* become human and natural, and only does so by destroying the human and natural substance it lives off. Capitalist artificiality seems limitless until limits reassert themselves, in the exploitation of labour (who rebels) as in the waste of resources (which finally hinders profitability). Humans will not become virtual. Online life is fascinating, a fascinating *myth*: neither world nor society can be completely spectacularised.

All these interpretations share a common misbelief: we would now be living under a *new capitalism*. According to its theorists, society has moved away from a factory-based economy toward a knowledge economy, communication is production, we are all worker-producers, exploitation is domination (and vice versa).

One may wonder how immaterial an Amazon warehouse or a container ship is.

What these theories really want to demonstrate is that this completely "new" capitalism is hardly *capitalist* anymore, since capital is diluted into social power mechanisms, every one of which comes under critical study, all of them except the one that structures the whole: wage-labour. There may be work left but no working class, rather a floating jobless population. As for a bourgeoisie, it is scarcely mentioned: the days of cosmopolitan jetsetting nomad finance oligarchs leave no room for such a simplistic notion as class. The wielders of economic power are everywhere and nowhere, the argument runs, so there is no bourgeois class anymore. Every critique is welcome, except the one that says there is a capital/labour relation embodied in two groups called "classes": that's old fashioned Marxism, dead and buried under the ruins of the Berlin Wall.

This was the mind-set alongside and against which the communisation concept was born.

§ 3: Excursus

The points made in this book derive from personal and collective experience, and there is no way of telling this story without telling our own. What we experienced was an example among others: we do not set ourselves as an example. This starting point will only come as a surprise to those who think it possible to negate their subjectivity and to consider communist theory (and themselves with it) as a pure and simple "product of class struggle."

3.1: Back to '68

A few words are useful on one of the small milieus that took part in the May–June '68 events and strike: Left Communists, libertarian communists, readers of the Situationist International (SI), anarchists . . . Some had been members of Pouvoir Ouvrier (Worker Power, a split from Socialisme ou Barbarie when this group casted off Marxism and class). One of the guys later involved in the RATP (Paris public transport) committee had thought of joining the SI or Socialisme ou Barbarie and finally preferred to stay out of both. This is not the place for a Situationist narrative, so let's just recall the link between the SI and SoB: Debord was a member of SoB for a year in 1960–61, and it was SoB which brought the worker councils theme to the SI. Fredy Perlman, active in the Citroën committee, had been critical of American academia and mainstream left, experienced Yugoslav socialism, and written on commodity fetishism. Members of the GLAT, another group in the German Left tradition, were also involved in the events we will retell. Most participants, however, did not belong to any formal gathering. They may have called themselves revolutionaries but were certainly not professional ones.[6]

What brought them together and enabled them to "naturally" connect with radical workers was their opposition to party and union bureaucracy, not as a bad leadership that ought to be replaced by a good one, but as something utterly antagonistic to worker interests and human emancipation. They also obviously regarded so-called socialist countries as capitalist. This may sound banal over twenty years after the collapse of the USSR, but it was not at a time when the vast majority of leftists supported some variant of Russian, Chinese, Cuban, Vietnamese, or Yugoslav socialism.[7]

As an illustration of the extent and limit of our understanding, I could mention the pamphlet that I wrote on the Russian revolution, published a couple of months before May '68.[8] Its purpose was to prove how the Russian proletariat had tried and failed to seize production and society into their own hands after 1917, before the Bolshevik party became the new exploiting class. Such a councilist interpretation fitted in with the theoretical framework common to our milieu: worker management extended to self-management of daily life (this last point demonstrating the influence of the SI).

3.2: The General Strike, an Eye-Opener[9]
Mid-May '68, a small worker minority, sometimes no more than a handful but often among the initiators of the strike in their plant, realised their inability to avoid union (usually the

Communist Party–led General Confederation of Labor) control over the strike. The only way for them to link with similar minorities was to step outside the workplace and go to occupied public buildings to meet like-minded people. Quite a few workers (young ones, particularly) would leave the factory to go and see "the students" (lots of whom never were university students), often to no avail, sometimes with a positive encounter. For two months, the Censier faculty in Paris (at the southern end of the Latin Quarter) was to be one of those meeting places that served as a coordinating organ for unelected but representative informal worker delegates (some from huge factories): a worker autonomy in search of itself. That experience was similar to others elsewhere and later, in Italy after 1969 for example, or in the Spanish *assembly movement* in the late '70s.[10]

Censier was not the only contact point for rebel proletarians, but was one of the very few that was able to organise common action against the bosses and police, and to counteract union power to some extent. The workers who came to Censier were not looking for people of good will ready to organise them or help them organise themselves. They needed neither masters nor servants, neither teachers nor disciples. They wanted to act with others (workers and nonworkers) as equals. Sociologically speaking, Censier was certainly one of the most "worker" loci in '68, albeit one where workerism was the least present. We did not try to level with the proles; we spoke to whoever was level with us.

The only ones who singled themselves out were diehard councilists: for fear of imposing the will of a minority upon the working class, the Informations et Correspondances Ouvrières (ICO) group played a very minor part in the committees and Censier general assembly meetings, and often met together in a separate room. Such behaviour confirmed what a year before the Situationists had called a "choice of nonexistence."[11]

Though we were not aware of it at the time, the events were to have a lasting impact on the common denominator of the radicals present at Censier. Because we believed in worker councils as a means to achieve self-management of everyday life, we stood for worker democracy, providing it was authentic (not manipulated by bureaucrats or politicians), and for self-management, providing it was generalised. This was indeed the prevailing mood in the Censier committees. But as it unfolded before our eyes, the reality of the strike went against this belief.

Initially, in many factories, without any formal decision-making meeting, a radical minority had imposed the work stoppage upon the majority. Later, as the strike went on, union officials had used debates and majority votes to wear out the movement. Democratic criteria such as proper expression of collective will, discussion prior to action, and majority control over decisions proved useless to understand the launching of the strike, let alone contribute to it. When faced with a minority act, no formal criterion would have been enough to determine if the minority was acting as a constraint upon the majority, or initiating an action supported by the general will. The same gesture (welding the factory doors, for example) took on a different meaning according to the circumstances.

When most of us (myself included, in my study of the failed Russian revolution) upheld worker democracy, it was not for the sake of renovating parliamentarianism, but because self-managing one's struggle was a necessary step on the way to self-managing production. Therefore, reexamining democracy led to question the priority usually given to the whole issue of management.

Besides, after the end of the general strike, and after the police reoccupied the Censier building, worker coordination lived on for over a year, in a very different way. In May–June '68, it had been commonly known as the "Censier committees" because of its location. When it gave itself the name *Inter-entreprises*, this reflected an inevitable regression: its prime function was now to connect factory struggles (a task far beyond its capabilities anyway). This fallback on work issues and a worker-focused vision of revolution were consistent with the implicit prevalent councilist state of mind, which some of us had started to question.

3.3 Maturation

Taking issue with worker power, we found ourselves a minority in the minority.

At the beginning of 1969, François Martin, one of the participants in Censier, drawing also from his work experience in a self-managed shoe factory in Algeria, started writing what was debated, altered, and published three years later.[12] He doubted that communist revolution would result from an accumulation of self-managed protests and strikes, quantity then turning into quality, first targeting the boss, then going deeper and deeper, attacking the police, the union, the politician, and the State, before finally doing away with wage-labour. François Martin argued that there was a gap between the breaking moment of any real strike or social unrest, the impetus that carries it forward, the breach it opens, and the closure when it ends, even if the strikers "have won." The (sometimes brief) self-organisation born out of the initial breakthrough depends on something else than itself. In other words, revolution is not a question of organisation, even of self-organisation. Self-organising is indispensable, but the ability and will to autonomy come from something else, and that "something" is the crux of communist theory.

"As soon as it has risen up, a class in which the revolutionary interests of society are concentrated finds the content and the material for its revolutionary activity directly in its own situation: foes to be laid low, measures dictated by the needs of the struggle to be taken; the consequences of its own deeds drive it on. It makes no theoretical inquiries into its own task." (*The Class Struggles in France*, 1850)

This Marx quote and similar ones were landmarks in our evolution: the "revolutionary programme" is *in the class*: the proletariat neither needs to be taught nor to educate itself.

This entailed reexamining a fundamental tenet of radical critique. The generation born under and against Stalinism had developed an anti-bureaucratic streak. "The fundamental problem of our time," *Socialisme ou Barbarie* declared in its first issue (1949), "is the nature of *worker* bureaucracy." In the analysis of Russian *bureaucratic capitalism*, its capitalist nature was deemed less important than its bureaucratic forms, which were supposedly capable of altering their basic nature. Anti-capitalism had morphed into anti-bureaucratism, which prioritised self-management, autonomy and democracy.

To preempt glib critique, let it be clear that we neither thought nor said: "Who cares if a minority decides, even against the majority, so long as the aim is right: destroying bourgeois power, profit, commodity!" Such an aim can only be achieved by the voluntary action of what the *Communist Manifesto* called "the immense majority." The withering of the State and economy will never be done top-down. To dot the i's, we had not turned "Bordigist." Bordiga justified Bolshevik dictatorship over the Russian proletariat in the name of a world revolution, which he hoped the Bolsheviks could promote from their Russian stronghold, while in fact Lenin and his party were managing the revolutionary failure. We rejected both dictatorship and democracy as political forms and thought a social revolution would do away with both.

François Martin was one of the first to state that in May '68 nearly everyone had stood for democracy, including the SI with its emphasis on council democracy. Of course direct horizontal generalised democracy differs from bourgeois parliamentarianism (or its contemporary forms: participatory, monitory democracy, etc.). But this is not the point. Democracy is an organisation form unable to create its content, and only the realisation of the content can achieve what democracy pretends to achieve, which is indispensable: circulating ideas, promoting debate, creating decision procedures, controlling delegates, and more.

Our line of thought addressed as much the Italian as the German-Dutch Left, as much Bordiga as Gorter or Pannekoek. Martin's angle had been the concrete process of class struggle. In 1969, our *Critique of Ultra-leftist Ideology* wondered how valid the Communist Left legacy was in relation to our experience.[13] It wished to make clear that communism is not wage-labour managed by the wage-labourers. Supposing autonomously organised masses took over of the productive forces, this would not be enough for these productive forces to lose their capitalist nature.

3.4 Portugal and Poland: Inextricable Problem and Solution

What we had been part of revived a provocative question hanging over us since the 1840s: class.

A few years later, two eminent European events helped us to think further. In Portugal (1974–75) though worker autonomy achieved a lot, it did not directly confront capital, and let itself be sidetracked, particularly via self-management. What was lacking was not more autonomy but endeavours and deeds that would have caused a break with capitalist basic laws and norms.

From the end of the 1970s and for more than ten years, the Polish working class was the main historical agent of the over-throw of the bureaucratic regime. This vividly demonstrated the continuing "centrality" of labour in modern society. At the same time, *class action* in Poland reanimated what was wrongly described as historically dead or powerless: the nation, the people (in the sense it had in nineteenth-century democratic revolutions), and a democracy that was able to renovate the State.

In Germany, in 1919, most proletarians had given at least passive support to a military counterrevolution led by a socialist government. But in Portugal and Poland, it was the action of the workers, including when they escaped union and party control, that opted for reform. However powerful it was, bureaucracy was not the Number One barrier. Bureaucrats only blocked the door to revolution because the proletarian kept or left the door closed.

Portugal and Poland, among other situations, forced to realise that the working class was as much the problem as the solution.

From then on, some, Jacques Camatte and *Invariance* especially, concluded that the proletarians had always acted and would always act as a constituent of capitalism.

Others, like us, thought the proletariat was a historical contradiction that only the proletarians were able to solve . . . if they did.

Without this background, the notion of communisation is incomprehensible.

CHAPTER 2

■ BIRTH OF A NOTION

§ 1: End of Classism

1.1: Classism in Crisis

We live in a class-structured world; therefore, the revolution that does away with classes will (a) take place on class grounds *and* (b) break with these class grounds.

Since the first half of the nineteenth century, critical theory has always run aground on this *and*.

Classism insists on *a* and ignores *b*. In the train of history, as a character says in the film *Snowpiercer*, all past revolutions have failed because the workers couldn't "take the engine" that drives society forward. And who better than the workers *can* take over the engine? Therefore, it is natural that classism should be *workerist*. It rarely pretends that only factory workers are proletarians, and simply adds other layers (office clerks, shop assistants, school teachers . . .) to manual labour. It will always refer to the statistics of labour worldwide, which belie the thesis of a global deindustrialisation: a lot more people are wage-labour now, and new factories keep being built.

All or most of this is true, and beside the point. The question is not the proportion of employed, semi-employed, or jobless workers in the world population but their relation and attitude to work.

Classism is the inevitable practice and theory of labour's struggle against capital, and it will persist as long as labour and capital coexist. A Chinese worker song said in the early 1920s: "Work shall be a pleasure, our offering to brotherhood.

We shall be called to it by the bells of liberty."[1] The lyrics sum up the ambiguity of proletarians hoping to liberate themselves by managing in their own interest the instrument of their enslavement.

The contradiction became visible in Italy after 1969 when two extremes met: an assertion of labour against capital which, though there was no general strike, went much further than in France or the United States in terms of autonomy and violence; and, most often by *the same* workers, a refusal of work, an anti-work attitude in the factory as well as in the neighbourhood. This was the underlying tendency that made the 1960s–70s significantly different from previous periods, though it involved a minority which never brought this clash of extremes to a point of no return. When proletarians chased the (communist-led) Italian General Confederation of Labour union leader out of Rome university in 1977, they were fighting an obvious but *exterior* enemy: communist insurrection would mean aiming at the target *within*, that is, abolishing oneself *as worker* and wage-labourer by initiating new nonmercantile and profit relations.

This perspective utterly befuddles classism and workerism, which explains why their theorisation has lost its dynamics. The last chapter of Steve Wright's classic study of Italian *autonomia*, *Storming Heaven*, is titled "The Collapse of Workerism."

Classism lives on as a political culture but its fulcrum has collapsed. Anti-classism or, worse, *no*-classism rules now: the *a* dimension, the fact that communist revolution will *take place on class grounds*, is denied or evaded. Before dealing with communisation, some of the various ways of tackling this thorny issue will help get to the heart of the matter.

1.2: Class Out of Fashion

A few decades ago, academics would often interpret the English and French revolutions of 1688 and 1789 as transitions from feudalism to capitalism, from aristocratic to bourgeois rule. Now mainstream and textbook history dissolves class factors into multicausality. When historians deny the existence of a bourgeoisie in France in 1789 on the grounds that it was ridden with too many diverging interests and conflicts to act as a social group, what is meant is that there cannot be any such thing as a bourgeois class in the twenty-first century either. This is reflected in radical politics, where issues multiply— such as those concerning gender, occupation, sex orientation, environment, race, age, and ethnic origin—and then have to be reconciled (intersectioning the sectioned, so to speak).

Some of the most acute theories of class dilution originated from lapsed Marxists, precisely ex-luminaries of Socialisme ou Barbarie: Cornelius Castoriadis was a forerunner of post-modernism, a notion popularised by another ex-SoB member, Jean-François Lyotard.[2] They were among the first to come up with a *post-worker* social doctrine. When Lyotard warned us in 1979 against the totalitarian risks involved in *grand narratives*, he did not mean the Bible or the Quran; he targeted the master narrative of the historical mission of the proletariat. The ascending bourgeoisie had claimed to bring prosperity, peace, and freedom, and we know what it meant. Likewise, so Lyotard argued, the proletarian pretension of emancipating humankind is a fraud. Marx's dream has led to a Stalinist nightmare. All we can do is hope for small narratives—fragmentary partial reforms.

Castoriadis and Lyotard excel at debunking the idea that the proletariat could and should replace the bourgeoisie: this was the only communist theory they ever knew. When Lenin said the workers would topple bourgeois governments and seize power, he meant the workers' representatives would do it, namely his party. When Socialisme ou Barbarie members said it, they meant the workers themselves. Unlike Lenin, they were genuine revolutionaries. Like Lenin, they mistook capital run by labour for communism. Revolution is not the workers taking over political power in order to run the economy.

As former revolutionary theorists drifted away from revolution, a parallel disorder hit the radical milieu. To lift up their spirits, radicals are prone to reading about present and past struggles. Paradoxically, in the 1970s, as the rebellious tide was ebbing, the opposite happened: the more was known about the history of modern revolutionary movements, the less revolutionary these endeavours seemed to some people. What started as a sound rejection of the golden proletarian legend, turned into the diametrically opposing view of workers who had consistently tried to ameliorate capitalism, glorified work, extolled progress and pressed for productivism. Warped logic was telling us that the more a group had emphasised the working class (for instance the Communist Workers' Party of Germany, KAPD), the closer to counterrevolution it had gone. Marcuse's famous thesis on the integration of the working class was carried one step further: the workers were now said to be integrated not by force or cunning but by their *own* action: the more they fought the boss, the more they locked themselves inside capitalist society. Castoriadis and Jacques Camatte (in different ways, of course) expounded at length on how capital and proletariat mutually need and breed each other. It is even repeated that narrow-minded working class is "reactionary" compared to enlightened middle class.[3]

Instead of debunking the legend of the heroic proletarian, one myth has been substituted for another.

1.3: The All-Inclusive Class (*Operaismo*)

Italian autonomists directly experienced the self-critique of work by a fraction of the working class, and they were a product of this practice. But as its main concern was political—that is, as it was looking for a way to mobilise and organise people—*operaismo* thought the work issue provided it with an efficient theme and slogan that was better adapted to modern times than those of the traditional worker movement. Quite simply, autonomia extended the world of work to the whole of society. Production no longer took place only on assembly lines: the "social factory" included the home, the street, school, prisons, hospitals . . . wherever capitalist society reproduced itself. As capital is everywhere, its antagonists are everywhere too: the proletarian is the Fiat metalworker and also the unemployed, the housewife, the student, the mental patient, the inmate, and others. If everybody is a worker, the watchword of the "political wage" or guaranteed income for all (originally launched by Potere Operaio) will bring together just about every sector of the population, minus the very top.

This raises the question of what production is, and of where value production comes from. Certainly not just from the assembly line: but not from everywhere either. The whole theory hinges on a play on the words *production* and *reproduction*. All or most elements of this society, from escorts to the Pope, contribute to its continuation, which can be called reproduction, so why couldn't what escorts and priests perform qualify as *labour*? Indeed why not (escorts are considered sex *workers*), but then we are not talking about surplus-value production anymore. If we are, we have to admit the difference between the workers on the Toyota assembly line and the media team broadcasting the six o'clock news. Strangely enough, the concept of *re*-production has been used to dissolve the concept of production . . .

. . . which operaismo does not really mind: one of its central planks is the growing *inessentiality* of work. If value is being produced everywhere, work is no longer vital to capital accumulation, and the ruling class maintains it as a means of control over the masses. Work has now been decoupled from value creation. Exploitation as analysed by Marx ("extracting more and more surplus value") would be now secondary to domination. A major Marxist shortcoming, autonomists say, is to overemphasise the economic aspect of capitalism and to neglect its (by far more important) sociopolitical dimensions.

Then why speak of classes? A *universal class* is a contradiction in terms: any class exists in relation and opposition to another. If there's a huge value circulating-producing class, it's not a class, it's a mass that encompasses nearly all of us (99 percent). If so, class analysis leads nowhere and is divisive, then let's talk about . . . what? Though many theorists dislike the word, the notion of a *people* epitomises rather well what Italian autonomists end up with.

The "minority in the minority" described in the previous chapter was only indirectly influenced by operaismo. What we drew from the Italian experience was the idea that we could not skirt the subject of *work*.

1.4 From Class to Individuals

Another answer to the worker movement and class dilemma was to think that capitalism produces proletarians that are potentially individual human beings.[4]

Capitalism is analysed as if it had already gone beyond its class structure. Its growth would no longer depend on profits derived from the exploitation of labour, but on the ability of value to valorise itself, with finance replacing manufacturing as the main business model. Like the autonomist school of thought, this theory believes that wage-labour persists not because it is necessary for the valorisation of capital, but as a social control mechanism.

The old proletarians/bourgeois class conflict endlessly fed on itself. Instead, we would now have a self-animated and self-valorised entity opposed by a potential union of individuals freed from class ties and available for a revolution "which can invoke . . . only human title." What Marx described in 1843 as the proletariat would already be created by capitalist evolution: "a class of civil society which is not a class of civil society . . . a sphere which has a universal character by its universal suffer-ing and claims no particular right because no particular wrong, but wrong generally, is perpetuated against it."[5] Capitalism (but is it still "capitalism" if the specific reality of *capital* has fused into other realities?) itself would have introduced the precondi-tion of communism which the proletarian individuals would only have to bring into effect.

This thesis would be relevant if capitalism *de-classised* itself, which it cannot do. It won't do the job for us. The "human title" is indeed the content of revolution, but it does not exist beforehand and will only emerge through an insurrectionary process. Capitalism does not do away with classes.

Still, the proletarian-individual theory points to an essen-tial dimension: communist revolution *does* go beyond class: if it does not, it either leaves the bourgeois in power, or creates a worker power that soon turns anti-worker. This theory has the merit of emphasising revolution as creation of the *social individual*. The community/individual couple is as difficult to express (standard words don't fit) as to experience, and its realisation is one of the components of communisation.

***

The purpose of this survey is not to demonstrate everybody was wrong, except for us. Only a roundabout approach could show what complexity we are dealing with. Not because everything is paradoxical but because "proletariat" is ambivalent: a class which is not a class, and whose action will do away with all classes. Each position we have summed up reflects a facet of reality.[6]

Despite their variations, most *class* concept rejecters pose that the capital/labour conflict can *only* be a conflict within capitalism, and this is where they are wrong. If we disagree with this adverb "only," it is not simply out of a will to believe in revolution but because that "only" is ahistorical. The decline of class perspective is mainly due to the defeat of the working class in the 1970s. And what of *blue-collar worker* renewed militancy in Asia? What about shantytown and *favela* people? They *are labour*. In fact, a great proportion of struggles now interpreted in ethnic, gender, or religious terms would have been labelled *class* conflicts forty years ago. Class is as much a reality as before, but "class" has been turned into a c-word. As Humpty Dumpty said in *Through the Looking Glass*, "in rather a scornful tone," when I use (or refuse) a word, "it means just what I choose it to mean."

§ 2: Facing the Conundrum

Ours was an effort to redefine class.

Defining wage-work is fairly easy, whether we look at a Volkswagen factory wage-worker with a relatively secure job in Wolfsburg, or at a Chinese *mingong*. Defining the wage-worker, however, is only relevant to us in so far as it helps define the proletarian and the proletariat, and here the trouble starts: we are not so sure anymore as to how wage-labour (and capital) could be destroyed. This was not a major dilemma for Marx, who by and large identified the proletariat with the working class. A century and a half after the *Communist Manifesto*, history tells us that, while there certainly is a connection between what classes (and particularly the wage-labour class) are in this society, and the way classes (and particularly the wage-labour class) will act in a communist revolution, the connection is not a "cause → effect" determination: the wage-worker (employed or not) has not often turned against wage-labour as a system. How could he or she collectively act as a revolutionary one day?

Nineteenth-century revolutionaries had insights of what a "kingdom of labour" would mean: universal *capitalism*: "The community is only a community of *labour*, and an equality of *wages* paid out by the communal capital—the *community* as the universal capitalist. Both sides of the relationship are raised to an *imagined* universality—*labour* as a state in which every person is put, and *capital* as the acknowledged universality and power of the community." (Marx, *1844 Manuscripts*, Section on Private Property and Communism)

A year later, Marx was even more explicit on the abolition of labour/work:

> It is one of the greatest misapprehensions to speak of free, human, social labour, of labour without private property. "Labour" by its very nature is unfree, unhuman, unsocial activity, determined by private property and creating private property. Hence the abolition of private property will become a reality only when it is conceived as the abolition of "labour" (an abolition which, of course, has become possible only as a result of labour itself, that is to say, has become possible as a result of the material activity of society . . .). An "organisation of labour," therefore, is a contradiction. The best organisation that labour can be

given is the present organisation, free competition. (*Notes on Friedrich List*, 1845)

This quote and similar ones illustrate the permanence of the contradiction mentioned above. Neither Marx nor (even less) Engels and their successors *directly* posed the question of how the working class would abolish work. For example, in Engels's explanation of how "labour created man himself," no distinction is drawn between *human activity* and *work*, which rules out all possibility of a critique of work.[7] As a consequence, revolution regenerates work, and socialism is a society organised around work.[8] Most of the time, when a complete change in productive activity and in the whole of social life was envisaged, it was supposed to come from more mechanisation, and in the twentieth century from automation.[9]

§ 3: The Common Good

Countless and varied visions of a future communist world have been suggested in modern times, by Sylvain Maréchal and Gracchus Babeuf, Marx, even Arthur Rimbaud in 1871,[10] Kropotkin and many anarchists, the Dutch council communists in the 1930s, and others.[11]

The common good or the community of goods! No more individual property in land: the land belongs to no one. We demand, we want, the common enjoyment of the fruits of the land: the fruits belong to all. (Sylvain Maréchal, *Manifesto of Equals*, 1796).

The first step to be taken then is to abolish a class of men privileged to shirk their duties as men, thus forcing others to do the work which they refuse to do. All must work according to their ability, and so produce what they consume—that is, each man should work as well as he can for his own livelihood, and his livelihood should be assured to him; that is to say, all the advantages which society would provide for each and all of its members. . . . The first step toward making labour attractive is to get the means of making labour fruitful, the Capital, including the land, machinery, factories, etc., into the hands of the community, to be used for the good of all alike, so that we might all work at "supplying" the real "demands" of each and all—that is to say, work for livelihood, instead of working to supply the demand of the profit market—instead of working for profit—i.e., the power of compelling other men to work against their will. (William Morris, *Useful Work v. Useless Toil*, 1884)

The wealth of the community: the land and the means of production, distribution and transport are held in common, production being for use and not for profit. . . . Full and complete Socialism entails the total abolition of money, buying and selling, and the wages system. It means the community must set itself the task of providing rather more than the people can use of all the things that the people need and desire, and of supplying these when and as the people require them. (Sylvia Pankhurst, "The Future Society," 1923)

What did communists suggest as a solution to the most severe economic crisis in history? In 1931, Otto Rühle wrote that the economy should "go back to its primitive role: provide all men with goods. They want bread in exchange for work . . . to adapt production to needs, this new form of economy must control the means of production. Hence the necessity of putting the means of production in the hands of the community."[12]

The way communism was envisaged could be summed up in the following equation:

communism =
direct democracy =
fulfilment of needs =
community + abundance =
equality

Since the future is envisioned as a self-organised human community, the big question is to know how it will organise itself. Who will lead: everybody, or nobody? How does the collective define itself? Will the human species delegate responsibilities to a few, and if it does, how?

It all comes down to what community we have in mind.

Here is the salient point: the way community is anticipated usually implies democracy.

For us, institution is not a priority, therefore neither is democracy.

We will not go back here to the critique of democracy, which we have dealt with in other essays,[13] and we will focus on one point: because the vast majority of revolutionaries (Marxists and anarchists) regard communism above all as a new way of organising society, they are first of all concerned by how to find the best possible organisational forms, institutions in other words, be they fixed or adaptable, complex, or extremely simple. (Individual anarchism is but another type of organisation: a coexistence of egos who can be free and equal because each is independent of the others.)

We start from another standpoint: communism concerns as much the *activity* of human beings as their *interrelations*. The way they relate to each other depends on what they *do* together. Communism organises production and has no fear of institutions, yet it is first of all neither institution nor production: it is activity.

§ 4: "Adieu to disappointment and spleen" (Jane Austen, *Pride and Prejudice*)

Marx was not the only ancestor in the making of the communisation concept.

The German-Dutch Left emphasised revolution as self-activity, and self-production of their emancipation by the exploited. Hence a rejection of all mediations: parliament, parties or unions. Without this, no revolution, no communisation.[14]

The Italian Left had insisted that revolution was not a question of organisation: getting rid of wage labour means doing away with money in all its forms, with value accounting, with the firm as a separate entity, with the economy as a specialised field of human activity. Quite a few people dismiss Amadeo Bordiga as an old fuddy-duddy or an inveterate Leninist: wrong on both counts. He was a contrarian, impervious to fashion, unconcerned by tardy recognition and it is difficult to slot him. He provided us with a jolt of clarity. Among other things, Bordiga was one of the very few who cared about ecology before it became a buzzword. Communism would not be a further "development of productive forces," but a *dis*-accumulation. "There is no fraud, however big it may be, that modern technology will refuse to endorse," he wrote in 1952. "Capitalism has long created a *technical* basis, viz. a heritage of productive forces which is enough for us . . . Even more so, capitalism has over-built." (*Politics and Construction*, 1952)[15]

Last but not least, the Situationist influence, often obscured by its (partly own) glitz. As the SI wrote in 1963, "The very core of the revolutionary project . . . is nothing less than the suppression of work in the usual present-day sense (and of the proletariat) and of all the justifications of previous forms of work." ("Ideologies, Classes, and the Domination of Nature," *Situationist International* no. 8, 1963)

What Bordiga and the Bordigists understood as a programme to be realised once bourgeois political power is smashed can only succeed, Situationists say, by the withering of commodity exchange, of the wage system, of the economy, by a transformation of all aspects of daily life from the very early insurrectionary days. Giving everyday life its real, broad sense, extending *worker* management to generalised *self*-management of daily life meant a qualitative leap beyond the councilist notion of worker management: if you modify the whole of life, then production, workplace, work and the economy cannot exist as separate domains anymore.

The German Left helped to see the *form* of the revolution, the Italian Left its *content*, and the SI the *process* that is the only way of obtaining that content.

§ 5: In a Nutshell

In substance: a revolution is only communist if it changes all social relationships into communist relationships, and this can only be done if the process starts at the beginning of the revolutionary upheaval. Money, wage-labour, the enterprise as a separate unit and a value-accumulating pole, work-time as cut off from the rest of our life, production for value, private property, State agencies as mediators of social life and conflicts, the separation between learning and doing, the quest for maximum and fastest circulation of everything—all of these have to be done away with and not just be run by collectives or turned over to public ownership. They must be replaced by communal, moneyless, profitless, stateless forms of life.

It is less a question of time (how long? how fast or slow?) than of *what* is done, by *whom*, and therefore *how*. In the very early days, the way the insurgents will treat workplaces, organise street fighting, feed themselves and relate to children, to give randomly chosen examples, will contribute to the future direction of events.

We would have nothing to object to the idea of a *transition* if it simply stated the obvious: communism will not be achieved in a flash. Yet concepts have a history, and "transition" implies a lot more than a transitory *moment*, something utterly different: a full-fledged transitory *society*.

However debatable Marx's *labour vouchers* are, at least his *Critique of the Gotha Programme* (1875) was trying to describe a society without money, therefore without wage-labour. His scheme of a time-based currency was supposed to be a provisional way of rewarding everyone according to their contribution to the creation of common wealth. Afterward, when Social Democrats and Leninists came to embrace the notion of transition, they forgot that objective, and their sole concern was the running of a planned economy.[16]

Communisation will not be *instantaneous*, but it will be *immediate* because it would not go through an intermediate period that is no longer capitalist but not yet communist, a period in which the working class would still work, not for profit or for the boss anymore, only for themselves, to go on developing the "productive forces" before being able to enjoy the then fully matured fruit of industrialisation. This is not the programme of a communist revolution. It was not in the past and it is not now. There is no need to go on developing industry, especially industry as it is now. And I am not writing this because of the ecology movement and the anti-industry trend in the radical milieu. As someone said forty years ago, half of the factories will have to be closed.

Such a deep and all-encompassing transformation as communism will span decades, perhaps several generations before it takes over the world. Until then, it will be straddling two eras and will remain vulnerable to internal decay or destruction from outside, all the more so as some areas may lag behind for a long time, and others go through temporary chaos. But the main point is that the communising process has to start as soon as possible. The closer to Day One the transformation begins and the deeper it goes from the beginning, the greater the likelihood of its success.

§ 6: If It's That Simple, Why . . . ?

Why has a "communising" prospect waited so long before becoming explicit?

At the dawn of capitalism, the 1830s and '40s were a time of farseeing communist insights. Marx's *1844 Manuscripts* probably expressed the sharpest edge of social critique, so sharp that the author himself did not think it necessary to circulate a text only published nearly a hundred years later (1932). Then, as the worker movement developed against a triumphant bourgeoisie, the communist intuition turned into demonstration and lost much of its visionary force. The 1848 *Communist Manifesto*'s concrete measures were compatible with radical bourgeois democracy, communism is only hinted at in *Capital* vol. 1 (1867), and the *Critique of the Gotha Programme* (1875) can hardly be regarded as communist. Though Marx never lost sight of communism, as is clear from his interest in the Russian *mir*, his critique of political economy came close to a critical political economy and a search for the "laws of history."[17]

The communist movement owes much to its time. In this early twenty-first century, we would be naive to believe that we are wiser than our predecessors because *we* realise how destructive productive forces can be. Just as the nature of capitalism is invariant, so are the nature and programme of the proletariat. This programme, however, cannot escape the situation and mind-set of each period.

At the end of the eighteenth century, in a country plagued with starvation and extreme inequality, and with very few factory workers, Babeuf advocated an egalitarian and mainly agrarian communism. His prime concern was to have everyone fed. It was inevitable for downtrodden men and women to equate the end of exploitation with a conquest over nature.

Fifty or a hundred years later, as industrial growth was creating a new type of poverty, joblessness and nonproperty, revolutionaries saw the solution in a worker-run "development of the productive forces" that would benefit the masses by manufacturing the essentials of life and free humankind from the constraints of necessity.

Marx is currently so often derided as a productivist that we must understand why he regarded the "Development of the Productive Forces as a Material Premise of Communism." This passage is worth quoting in full:

> This "alienation" (to use a term which will be comprehensible to the philosophers) can, of course, only be abolished given two practical premises. For it to become an "intolerable" power—a power against which men make a revolution—it must necessarily have rendered the great mass of humanity "propertyless," and produced, at the same time, the contradiction of an existing world of wealth and culture, both of which conditions presuppose a great increase in productive power, a high degree of its development. And, on the other hand, this development of productive forces

(which itself implies the actual empirical existence of men in their world-historical, instead of local, being) is an absolutely necessary practical premise because without it want is merely made general, and with destitution the struggle for necessities and all the old filthy business would necessarily be reproduced; and furthermore, because only with this universal development of productive forces is a universal intercourse between men established, which produces in all nations simultaneously the phenomenon of the "propertyless" mass (universal competition), makes each nation dependent on the revolutions of the others, and finally has put world-historical, empirically universal individuals in place of local ones. Without this, (1) communism could only exist as a local event; (2) the forces of intercourse themselves could not have developed as universal, hence intolerable powers: they would have remained home-bred conditions surrounded by superstition; and (3) each extension of intercourse would abolish local communism. Empirically, communism is only possible as the act of the dominant peoples "all at once" and simultaneously, which presupposes the universal development of productive forces and the world intercourse bound up with communism. Moreover, the mass of propertyless workers—the utterly precarious position of labour-power on a mass scale cut off from capital or from even a limited satisfaction and, therefore, no longer merely temporarily deprived of work itself as a secure source of life—presupposes the world market through competition. The proletariat can thus only exist world-historically, just as communism, its activity, can only have a "world-historical" existence. World-historical existence of individuals means existence of individuals which is directly linked up with world history. (*German Ideology*, Part I, A, § 5)

A century later, *ecology* is the in-word. Nobody seriously believes in a factory-induced or a worker-managed paradise, new public orthodoxy declares the industrial dream to be a nightmare, so there is little merit in refuting the techno-cult or advocating renewable energy or green building.

The idea of communisation as a revolution that creates *communism*—and not the *preconditions* of communism—appears more clearly when capitalism rules over everything, extensively in terms of space (the much-talked-about globalisation), and intensively in terms of its penetration into everyday life and behaviour. That is the best possible answer to the inevitable question Why talk of communisation *now*?

One might wonder why "communisation" hardly surfaced in Italy in 1969–77, when the country came close to breaking point. Part of the answer is likely to be found in the reality of Italian worker autonomy, in theory as in practice. Operaism emphasised more the revolutionary "subject" or agent than the content of the revolution, so the content finally got reduced to autonomy itself. As explained in § 1.3, that was linked to the limits of operaismo, whose goal was to create or stimulate organisation (top-down, party-led, or bottom-up, council-based, depending on which autonomia group we look at). This may be the reason why a wealth of practical communist critiques and endeavours resulted in so little synthetic theorisation of communisation. Apart from such hypotheses, it would be risky to embark on sweeping generalisations purporting to explain the (mis)adventures of theory in a particular country by the ups and downs of class struggle in that country. There is little fun in playing the prophet of the past.

§ 7: The Word

In English, the word has been used for a long while, to convey something very different from what we are dealing with here. *To communise* was often a synonym for *to sovietise*, that is, to implement the full program of the communist party in the Leninist (and later Stalinist) sense.[18]

More rarely, *communisation* has been used as a synonym for radical *collectivisation*, with special reference to Spain in 1936–39, when factories, farms, rural and urban areas were run by worker or peasant collectives. Although this is related to what we mean by communising, most of these experiences invented local currencies or took labour-time as a means of barter. These collectives functioned as worker-managed enterprises, for the benefit of the people, yet enterprises all the same.

This was not communisation.

It is uncertain who first used the word with the meaning this book is interested in. To the best of our knowledge, it was Dominique Blanc: orally in the years 1972–74, and in writing in *Un Monde sans argent* (A World without Money), published in three booklets in 1975–76 by the OJTR, the same group that also published *Militancy, the Highest Stage of Alienation.*[19] *Un Monde sans argent* said the difference between communist revolution and all variants of reformism was not that revolution implied insurrection, but that this insurrection would have to start communising society . . . or it would have no communist content. In that respect, *Un Monde sans argent* remains a pivotal essay.

Talking of words, we hardly have the vocabulary adequate for our perspective: "The words at our disposal to describe a society did not foresee that this society could be communist." (Bruno Astarian)[20]

But first, more on *work*.

CHAPTER 3

■ WORK UNDONE

Road Work Unreal

In 1997, in a backwater in Sarthe (Western France), a few dozen men could be seen on a roadwork crew supervised by a team leader employed by a big construction firm. After two months, the man was arrested, as it turned out that nobody had ordered the roadwork, part of which was still finished and financed as he had convinced banks and public agencies that the project was genuine. Between 1983 and 1996, Philippe Berre had been sentenced fourteen times for starting up phony construction work. In 2009, a film fictionalised the event and showed Berre in a favourable light as a transient miracle man who briefly brought jobs and hopes to the unemployed.[1]

Berre's motivation was not money but rather the urge to *do*, to feel useful, to lead a work team. In 2010, he did it again as part of the rescue operation after the Xynthia storm that killed over fifty people in the West of France.

Berre is a fictitious boss, an antihero of our time, a cunning manipulator of human resources, a nomad who sleeps in his car, as mobile as his parasitic activity, living off dreams, a perfect illustration of contemporary rootless flow. Money circulates but few accumulate it, success has no future, industry builds the useless, communication and virtuality are paramount. Lack of reality is quite common; Berre just lacks respectability.

When it takes a con man to bring jobs, income, self-respect and "meaning" to a decaying community, even if it happens to prove a short-lived fallacy, this forces us to wonder what the economy and work really mean. The unemployed locals trusted Berre because he was providing them with more than jobs and money: he was bringing them socialisation, a role, a social status and recognition. What is useful? useless? fictitious? profitable or not? Was that bit of motorway more, less, or equally absurd than thousands of miles of "real" tarmac? What work is social waste? Beyond the hard fact of the materiality of work (it creates things, brings in income and is often unpleasant), we have to explore the reality and *unreality* of work.

First, what do we mean by *work*?

§ 1: Working Substance

Though radical critique has a natural interest in history and prehistory, it cannot ground itself in an understanding of the past. Defining capitalism by what we think we know of its origins, and going further and further back to the dawn of humankind, leaves us with a definition that will have to change according to changes in historical studies. No science is neutral: anthropological methods and findings reflect their time. Marx and Engels relied a lot on Lewis H. Morgan and Johan J. Bachofen. Later Wilhelm Reich found his views on sexuality confirmed by Bronislaw Malinowski's ethnography. Forty years ago, Marshall Sahlins was avidly read by libertarian communists. Now other approaches and theses are coming to the fore.

Work is a historical category but *cannot be defined by its history*. Its genealogy may be fascinatingly stimulating: it will not explain its logic.

Marx's essential concepts of wage-labour and work (in his early writings as well as in *Capital*) did not depend on (pre) historical research. Engels's later dealings with origins do not provide us with the most acute perception of what work is.[2]

The questions of "primitive communism"—gift, potlatch, the *kula* ring, "abundance or scarcity in primitive societies," whether hunter-gatherers worked or not, or when work as such emerged—have their own validity; we will not venture on that field.[3] Our subject is societies where we can see the features that constitute work, bearing in mind that its characteristics have only fully matured for a few centuries.

We wish to define work with a definition that is *as abstract as possible*.

As any social analysis implies a delineation of what is specific to the human species, it is best to make it explicit and . . . minimal: as Oscar Wilde wrote in 1891, "the only thing that we really know about human nature is that it changes."[4] It changes because humans contribute to producing our own conditions: we cannot alter ourselves at will but, for better or worse, evolve as we make our environment evolve. As they produce their material conditions of life, human beings do a lot more: production means social interaction, talking, travelling, and more. We coproduce ourselves, treating ourselves and our own activity as objects, as something different from us, which we reflect upon and modify: we are both *subject* and *object*. Humans have a history and can distance themselves from themselves (and therefore can alienate themselves). This involves choice and freedom (and possible loss of freedom).

That objectification contains the possibility of work.

1.1: Work Is Class

For that potential to become effective, there has to be a surplus product, and one that is more than mere reserves (food stores, for instance): it has to be a surplus used to free members of society from the obligation of producing for themselves, and enabling them to produce for others. Work is a relationship between *labour* and *surplus labour*: there is a separation between the expenditure of energy necessary for workers' subsistence and the expenditure of physical and mental effort beyond that subsistence, which results in a surplus product. Society divides between a working group and a nonworking group that takes hold of the production of the first group. Even when workers remains in control of the means of production and organises their activity themselves, the result is no longer theirs. Work is social division.

There is no work without surplus labour, which a minority takes up for itself.

1.2: Work Reduces Every Activity to a Common Substance

Human activity began to take the form of *work* when humankind, over thousands of years and in places we will never know, came to the stage when a number of productive acts (probably very few at the beginning) ceased to be performed, lived, and perceived for what each of them specifically was and resulted in: for example, flour or cloth. From then on, that flour and that cloth existed above all for what they had in common: though they differed in nature, both were comparable effects of human effort, which could be reduced to a universally quantifiable element, the average exertion of physical and mental energy necessary to produce that amount of flour or that piece of cloth. From then on, these two objects were made *because of* what they had in common: it is this universal corresponding substance we call *value*.

Another decisive change happened with the shift from the exchange of a commodity for another (flour for cloth), aiming at fulfilling two needs, to a very different kind of exchange, aiming not at getting a specific object (flour or cloth) but *money*, which enables us to buy any possible item or can be saved or invested.

Money is crystallised labour: it gives value a recognizable form.

Money was not born out of practical necessities, for example to make barter easier, like a simpler means of swapping an amount of flour for a piece of cloth without any swapper "losing" in the bargain. Credit and debt predated money, as proved by the masses of indebted farmers in ancient times.

Whatever the origin, work and money have become inseparable. Money materialises (even in the dematerialised forms of plastic money and online accounts) the way activities relate to each other, human beings to each other, and classes to each other.

Value manifests itself in the act of exchange, but it originates in work.[5]

1.3: Wage-Labour Turns Work into a Commodity

With wage-labour, work is not simply activity for money: it is itself bought and sold.

With the general selling and buying of labour power, for the first time in history, social classes are directly determined by their members' respective role (bourgeois or proletarian) in production.

This essential fact, however, is perceived through a glass, darkly. First, the extension of wage-labour (even the CEO works) blurs the worker/nonworker opposition. Second, two or three billion under- or unemployed billion people seem to belong to a "wageless" class, whereas they are indeed part of the world wage system, even if *at best* they only get casual jobs.

The tendency to universalise wage-labour creates an entirely new situation, including where and when labour power remains unemployable. The slave, serf, and tenant farmer's sole perspective was to remove the fetters embodied in the person of the slave-owner, lord, or landowner, and then to work free from moneymakers, taxmen, rulers, and other parasites. Today's computer factory operatives or cash-crop field labourers can only emancipate themselves by putting an end to work as such, as the commodity that reproduces all other commodities. The perspective is no longer a liberation *of* work, but *from* work: work is what turns activity into labour power for sale, and negates human capacity except as labour power.

1.4: Work Is Separation

Work is the form taken by the production of the material conditions of life when the activity to produce them has been cut off from other activities, not to the same extent of course today in Manhattan and in an African village. Modern wage-labour carves up time into categories such as work, school, leisure, holiday, unemployment, and retirement, and splits space between places to earn a living, to eat and sleep, to shop, to have fun, and so on.

The nonwork time-space (as different from work time) is not a capitalist creation: it has coexisted with work since work appeared. The capitalist novelty is to push the separation to extremes, as it develops more intensively and extensively the difference between productive (of value) and unproductive.

The growing domination of work over society cannot fail to have an effect on the play/work relation. What we call play is never free from social constraints (dolls for girls, cowboy outfits for boys), and in our society it is often work-related. Meccano all-metal parts used to fit in with the factory-oriented mechanical mind-set. In the computer age, nuts and bolts look boring when the child only has to press keys to make something happen on a screen: kids and adults use as toys the same tools that organise the office and the shop floor. We won't do away with work by extending the scope of the playworld. Work and play will be overturned at the same time.[6]

1.5: Work Is Productivity and Accountancy

Work is based on the difference between necessary labour and surplus labour, and capital is made of competing firms: each company is a pole of value seeking optimum growth and doing its best to increase surplus labour at the expense of necessary labour. Productivity and standardisation are inherent to work: the hunt for the most efficient way of lowering production costs leads to periodic changes in the work process: "developing the productive forces" is a *consequence* of wage-labour. Work and value (each supporting the other) cause production for production's sake—in fact, for *value*'s sake—and therefore productivism and planned obsolescence.

Today, objects are constantly compared and exchanged according to the average labour time they are supposed to incorporate: consequently, human beings are also estimated and treated in the same way.

1.6: Work Is Reducing Everything to a Minimum of Time

Value is time and production is ruled by time, that is, by productivity.

With the ascension of capitalism, exchange stopped being based on comparing the average social necessary time of two or more productions: society as a whole tends to base most exchanges on an average of minimal working times of most producers.

The best way to make the expenditure of energy as productive as possible is to quantify the time it takes, in order to shorten this time. Time-counting lies at the heart of value. This is why separating work from the rest of life is essential: one can only measure a moment and the physical or mental effort exerted during that moment, if that segment of time is distinct from the others. Some nineteenth-century factories would lock the gate to prevent workers from leaving. Work is a struggle against time.

A middle-class housewife roughly knows how much to pay her cleaning lady: knowing how much her *own* housework is "worth" would be meaningless. Even if both persons performed exactly the same tasks from nine to twelve, these 180 minutes would have a very different reality for the wage-earner who comes in for a three-hour service, and the housewife who is busy vacuuming while keeping the house in a variety of ways. Work is paid quantified activity.[7]

The piece-rate wage of a worker operating alone on a machine will be calculated according to the number of seconds necessary to perform a prescribed set of movements.

Money is crystallised labour, but it only functions as an instrument of circulation because commodities relate to each other via their prices, and a price does not tell us the exact amount of labour time incorporated in a given commodity, viz. the specific quantity of energy expended by the worker who produced it. Nor does it have to. The bourgeois cares about profit, not value.

Like the stopwatch time-and-motion studies of yesterday, today's computerised management is based on averages. Though the bourgeois does everything he can to individualise each work station and each pay, "piece rate" is only possible when workers produce items on their own, or perform a task on their own (like a supermarket cashier), on a specific machine the separate output of which is measurable. As most work processes involve cooperation, the assembly line for example, this is rarely the case. Moreover, in England 1973–74, the three-day week (instead of five) caused by the coal miners' strike resulted in a production loss less than the expected two-fifths. This proved the existence of an untapped stock of productivity, because in normal circumstances a worker succeeds in doing less than required for what he or she is paid. No scientific management can reduce work to a quantified amount, nor eliminate labour resistance: those who do the job never totally lose control over it.

Nevertheless, what a sociologist once called Taylorism's "rational madness" suits capital's needs. When the manager of a mouse pad factory introduces new machinery to force a worker to produce more for the same pay, he can never exactly quantify how much more profitable this worker is going to be (whereas the manager knows that the mouse pad will be sold $1.05 in the shop), but this pressure results in the worker being more productive and bringing in more profits. What matters to business is prices, in the form of wages and profits. A capitalist does not know what *value* is, yet he cares about it in the forms of profit, interest, or rent.

The capitalist fight against time is the ultimate cause of planned obsolescence and of time-saving obsession in daily life. Both phenomena have reached unprecedented heights in the last thirty years: no need here to dwell on them.

Human emancipation implies putting an end to time constraint over productive activity, that is, an end to productivity.

***

For clarity's sake, we have set apart six elements which combine to make work what it is. They have not been presented in chronological order: once again, we do not pretend to explain the historical origin of work. All we know is that these features did not acquire equal status at the same time: it took millennia for exchange to be ruled by true *equivalents*, viz. according to a fairly valid reckoning of necessary labour time. Besides, "money" in the sense of counting in value terms, and producing and circulating goods as equivalents, predated money in the form of coins, notes, checks, and other instruments that only fulfil that function and are not used for everyday or ritual purposes. Coinage is fairly recent, dating from the seventh century BC or earlier.

The important thing is that each of these six features has now become a condition of the others. For example, to force men and women to "earn a living" as wage-earners, they have to be deprived of autonomous means of existence, and measuring work implies separating it from the rest of life. Only modern capitalism fully develops these elements into a whole that constitutes work as such.

1.7: Under the Rule of Work

Our aim is the best possible abstract definition of work, but we are not aiming at work in general, only at work as it exists: nowadays work *is wage-labour*. Though only a minority of the world population receives a wage, and a still smaller minority enjoys a proper work contract (with labour rights, social contributions, possibly union dues), wage-labour determines other forms of work.

Capitalist forms determine precapitalist ones. The seven-year-old Turkish girl who looks after her parents' herd of sheep contributes (even marginally) to her family's income. Meanwhile in the nearby town, her younger brother is paid a wage as a casual labourer, and the elder brother is a migrant worker in Germany, where the girl herself might emigrate later to get a job as a hotel cleaner. Her family life is part of the global reproduction of capital/labour relations. The world market ever draws new people into the ambit of capitalism, a small portion of Earthlings now live a purely "subsistence economy" life, and work and money penetrate the recesses of shantytowns.

The question is which viewpoint is chosen. For a sociologist or an anthropologist, the Turkish girl's activity is still "embedded" within precapitalist relations, and he will point out that her kinship ties are still suffused with archaism (the prospect of an arranged marriage for instance), which is true. But if we wish to understand the reality of work, we can only emphasise the commonality between that young girl and a Chinese miner or a Bolivian office clerk (this does not mean that all three have the same impact upon the course of history).

The dominant social relationship is not the only one that exists, but all others are determined by it, including volunteer unpaid activity (enabled by money-earning work) and slavery (forced, unpaid work with bosses exercising total control over workers, which today concerns an estimated twenty to thirty million people).

Wage-labour is central, and work remains the big social integrator, the one on which all others (family, ethnicity, religion, etc.) depend. Capitalism regulates the whole of society, including the "backward" elements it carries along.[8]

§ 2: Neither Work nor Economy

§ 1 aimed at identifying six characteristics of work: necessary labour/surplus labour, and class division; value; wage-labour as labour power turned commodity; separation; productivity and accountancy; and time-saving. Just to be clear, our definition abstractly differentiated between categories that in reality are intertwined. We are not constructing a theoretical engine that would stop functioning if one of its parts was missing.

To grasp the possible link between capitalism and a revolution that would abolish work, instead of considering the six components separately, this section will now consider them in their unity.

2.1: Production Is Not Economy

"Production" is often thought of as craft and industry, an activity which results in something being *made*: a car, a teacup, a movie.... We should rather speak of production each time means of labour are applied to raw material to transform it into a consumable item different from what it used to be. This is true with agriculture, but also with gathering, hunting, and fishing, which use tools and weapons and involve cooperation and knowledge.

Yet economy is not a synonym for production.

The riddle is to understand that the production of material conditions of life has become a reality called the economy, first different from, then gradually separated from the rest of life, until much later it came to dominate the whole of life.

When and how? ... Let us just say that there is no such thing as "economic history" from 100,000 BC to the twenty-first century: the economy is a historical artefact that has not existed everywhere at every time. Capitalism is not the only system where work and economy exist and thrive, but they did not have the same sway over society in ancient Athens as they do in Greece today.

Economic thought prioritises production and distribution of goods. Socialists want to produce and distribute in a useful fair manner. To allow for resources to be renewed, ecologists want the economy to take into account natural data. In both critiques, the postulate remains economic: how to *adjust needs to resources.*

You can tell an economist by his main concern: not the relationship between human beings, but how they produce.

To him, the connection between necessary labour and surplus labour is the obvious starting point: "We need to produce if we want to eat, to have a place to sleep, to cure the sick." First the necessities of life, then the superfluous. Usefulness before fun. Bread before music. Capitalism has always advertised itself as the best possible production system in the ultimate general interest. Socialist and communist doctrines aim at the same target, albeit collectively decided, by methods which respect humans (by maximum automation, or by a return to local community craft and agriculture), leaving everybody enough time to cultivate their mind and body after attending to productive tasks.

The flaw is to start from the necessity of satisfying vital requirements. With no food, I die: that undeniable fact is only meaningful in relation to the other equally important fact that human existence is social. I do not eat first, only to enter society afterward. Hunger is always experienced and dealt with in connection with how people live, whether in Alaska or Tahiti. That second factor does not come on top of the first: they are one. Extreme cold is no more *the* cause of the Inuits' social organisation than tropical humidity is *the* cause of the Tahitians' social organisation. No vital necessity has priority over social links: both act simultaneously. This applies to capitalism. And to communism: except production will not be playing the same role.

Our question is not: How do people produce? Nor even: What do they produce (books or bombs)? But: What part does production have in human life?

Radicals often say that our objective is not to produce for production's sake but to reach a minimum level of abundance under which no emancipation would be feasible.

Conversely, others regard frugal moderation as a prerequisite of freedom and solidarity. In Ursula Le Guin's 1974 novel *The Dispossessed*, the rather libertarian mode of life on planet Anarres owes a lot to a tough climate that favours mutual help and discourages accumulation.

In both visions, whether the emphasis is on abundance or sobriety, priority remains to manage production and distribution. Both ignore the fact that the abundance/want duality is an economic category, to be addressed as such.

2.2: Communism as Activity

Prevailing socialist or communist views blame capitalism for mass manufacturing goods without caring *first* for real needs. To avoid this, communists usually proposes to *start* from needs, real and collectively agreed upon needs, and to fulfil them by democratised self-managed organisation and fair distribution, without the mediation of a market.[9]

This is neglecting that need is another economic category, based upon the separation between an individual and something he lacks. Abstract needs go together with abstract beings that we are shaped into by the prevalence of the economy.

There is no denying that the satisfaction of elementary necessities has to be achieved according to existing resources. Marx is sometimes remembered for having "discovered the law of development of human history: the simple fact, hitherto concealed by an overgrowth of ideology, that mankind must first of all eat, drink, and have shelter and clothing, before it can pursue politics, science, art, religion, etc." (Engels's speech at Marx's funeral, 1883).

Unfortunately, "law" becomes fallacy if it turns into the belief that human life consists above all in satisfying needs, and therefore that revolution should consist above all in creating a society where needs would be satisfied (first the indispensable, later the superfluous). Humans only fulfil (or fail to fulfil) their needs in a nexus of interrelations. It takes exceptional circumstances for us to eat with the sole purpose of not dying of hunger. For a human being, eating is always more than eating. We usually eat in (chosen or unchosen) company, we decide to eat on our own, or we are forced to. We often follow a (healthy or not) diet. We skip lunch. We overeat. This is true of all vital activities.

Contrary to popular belief, the "materialist conception of history" does not claim that "the economy" rules history. This is how the first part of *German Ideology* is often misread, but the point made by Marx is quite different:

> History: Fundamental Conditions . . .
>
> The first premise of all human existence and, therefore, of all history, [is] . . . that men must be in a position to live in order to be able to "make history." But life involves before everything else eating and drinking, a habitation, clothing and many other things . . .
>
> The second point is that the satisfaction of the first need (the action of satisfying, and the instrument of satisfaction which has been acquired) leads to new needs; and this production of new needs is the first historical act.
>
> The third circumstance which, from the very outset, enters into historical development, is that men, who daily remake their own life, begin to make other men, to propagate their kind: the relation between man and woman, parents and children, the family. (*German Ideology*, Part I, A)

In other words: (a) social evolution depends on how we produce our material conditions of life (and not for example on how we see the world); (b) we produce these material conditions in connection with others (and in class societies, via class relationships).

There is no technical (or environmental) determinism or fatality: neither the wooden plough, the steam engine, nor the computer cause the course of history. The "materialist conception of history" does not suggest that economy would be history's prime mover. It explains why the present domination of the economy is a historical phenomenon. Productive forces (as defined at the beginning of § 2.1) are the basis of any society: only under capitalism does their systematic growth become the main social determinant.

Our concern is not to invent the society that will match needs and resources (as economists would have it), or turn artificial extravagant needs into reasonable ones (as ecologists would prefer). Let's understand elementary needs for what they are. Marx was not the first to remark that the main human need is the need for other humans. The need to eat is inseparable from the need for the other being, and both needs are (or are not) satisfied at the same time.

Revolutionary times confirm this: the insurgent proletarian has "no reserve," no money, no food, nor (at the very beginning) any weapon, and his or her only asset is the ability to interact with other proletarians.

Under the pressure of circumstances, the insurgents will sometimes be forced to organise some form of rationing. Yet revolution would fail if it proved incapable of drawing a line between its fundamental programme and contingency measures. If emergencies happened to dictate the programme, we would be doomed.

Revolutionary action will not be fuelled by the best or most equal way of distributing goods, but by the human links and the actions that spring from them. In communisation, activity prevails over its productive result, because that result depends on the impetus and the links that the insurgents will be able to create among themselves.

"This is sheer idealism," a reader might object: "Production is not a question of social links but of consistent effort and appropriate equipment, especially when one billion people are underfed!" Or, to quote the minutes of the Central Soviet Executive Committee meeting on November 17, 1917, "what socialism implies above all is keeping account of everything."

The objection misunderstands what social life is.

What motivates insurgent proletarians (even the hungry ones) is not the need to feed themselves but to associate with fellow proletarians, which—among other effects—will enable them to eat. The necessity to produce food, to grow carrots for instance, will be met via *social relations* which, *among other activities*, will grow vegetables (this does not mean that every minute of horticulture will be fun). This will be true of "poor" countries as well as of "rich" ones.

Counterrevolution will naturally exploit inevitable disorders and local shortages. Revolution will not face the challenge by developing hyperefficient industry, nor will it get rid of bourgeois armies by a stronger military build-up. It will be neobureaucrats who will present themselves as "practical" minds and argue that insurrectionary spontaneity must give way to productive organisation (surely with participatory democracy).

In return for a few significant changes (ending nuclear energy, for example), "common sense" will be telling us that a hammer or a laptop is neither capitalist nor communist, that technique is neutral and therefore good when properly used. In fact, when "realists" talk of efficiency, they promote productivity, with the implicit "no pain, no gain" motto. Productivity and work go together. Work standardises. Counting time spent in production implies separating production from the rest of time, hence splitting apart from life a distinct moment called work. Revolution cannot make timesaving one of its priorities.

The division of labour will not be superseded simply by redistributing tasks, with everyone alternating between plumbing in the morning, gardening in the afternoon, childminding today and cooking tomorrow. Neither does cooperation abolish work as such: working *together* does not abolish work. Nor does a two-hour working day. Replacing private by community producers is only communist if the products are not compared (therefore are not produced and used as comparable) between themselves according to the (explicit or implicit) calculation of the (real or alleged) average labour time to produce them. If such a comparison did occur, it would also compute these activities and with them the people involved: sooner or later social life would be centred on *productivity*, and value would resurface, however fraternal the community might wish and try to be.

Work and value go together and each supports the other. Communism is not the substitution of even the most democratic *planning* to capitalist "anarchy." Supposing all companies were managed as one company but labour-time accounting still prevailed, it would only be a new form of capitalism, and *work* would still exist.

*****

What is the most damning indictment against capitalism? Wherever wage-labour rules, free time is a time that proletarians have to buy through their work, before being able to *afford* their freedom afterward, when they consume objects and enjoys leisure paid for by their wage. It is this separation, and everything that goes with it (each person faces another as a means or a competitor) that communisation will have to do away with. Abject misery, in the nineteenth or twenty-first century, in twenty-first-century London or Bombay, is only one aspect of this process, the most terrible one.

This chapter started with a fictitious boss offering deceptive jobs, and workers building a nowhere road. Philippe Berre made people live in a dream: how *real* is our world? Some people earn a living by inventing advertising material, others by printing it, or putting it into mail boxes, disposing of it, recycling waste paper into more junk mail, while experts are paid to comment upon the whole thing, and so on. Surrealists wondered whether we suffered from a deficit or an excess of reality. But work will not disappear because it is deemed obnoxious or absurd. The mere pressure of its internal contradictions will not make it explode and will not create on the shop floor or in the office some new reality resembling the *generic activity* theorised by Marx in the 1840s.

Work will never self-destroy.

CHAPTER 4

■ CRISIS OF CIVILISATION

All historical crises are crises of social reproduction. We will try to investigate how the present crisis, like *and unlike* others in the past, forces society to face the contradictions that formerly stimulated its dynamics but now drive it into a critical juncture.

Every major crisis forces social groups to come to grips with the deep contradictions of society. In capitalism, class confrontation is the prime mover that drives society forward: it forces the bourgeoisie to adapt to labour pressure, to "modernise." Crisis is when these formerly positive pressures strain the social fabric and threaten to tear it apart.

Contradiction does not mean impossibility. Up to now, all big crises have ended in the system managing to pull through and eventually becoming more adaptable and protean. No "ultimate" crisis is automatically contained in even the most acute contradictions.

§ 1: Why "Civilisation"?

Capitalism is driven on by a social and productive dynamism, and by an unheard-of regenerative ability, but it has this weakness: by its very strength, by the human energy and the technical power it sets into motion, it wears out what it exploits, and its productive intensity is only paralleled by its destructive potential, as proved by the first civilisation crisis it went through in the twentieth century.

No value judgement is implied here. We do not oppose *civilised* people to *savages* (even good or noble ones) or *barbarians*. We do not celebrate "great civilisations" which would have been witness to the progress of humankind. On the other hand, we do not use the word in the derogatory sense it has with writers like Charles Fourier, who called "civilisation" a modern society plagued by poverty, trade, competition, and the factory system. Neither do we refer to those huge geohistorical sociocultural constructs known as Western, Judeo-Christian, Chinese, or Islamic civilisations.

The *civilisation* we speak of does not replace the notion of mode of production. It merely emphasises the scope and depth of a world system that tends to be universal, and is also capable of disrupting and then reshaping all kinds of societies and ways of life. The hold of wage-labour and commodity over our life gives them a reality and dynamics that were unknown in the past. Capitalism today is the only all-encompassing network of social relationships able to expand geographically and, with the respective differences being considered, to impact on Jakarta as well as Vilnius. The spread of a world capitalist way of life is visible in similar consumer habits (McDonald's) and architecture (skyscrapers), but its deep cause is in the dominance of value production, of productivity, of the capital-wage labour couple.

The concept of a *mode of production* is contemporary to capitalism. Whether or not Marx invented the phrase, it has become common since the nineteenth century because capitalism imposes on us the image of factors of production combined to beget a product or a service bought or sold on a market, and of a society ruled by supply/demand and productivity.

Then the concept was retrospectively applied (often inadequately) to other systems, past and present: the *Asiatic* or the *domestic* mode of production.[1] Whatever relevance these derivations have, they pay tribute to the overwhelming presence of the *capitalist* mode of production.

Capitalist civilisation differs from empire, which has a heart, a core, and when the core withers and dies, the whole system around it goes too. On the contrary, capitalism is a polycentric world system with several rival hegemons, which carries on as a global network if one of the hegemons expires. There is no longer an inside and an outside as with Mesopotamian, Roman, Persian, Hapsburg, or Chinese empires.

A crisis of civilisation occurs when the tensions that formerly helped society to develop now threaten its foundations: they still hold but they are shaken up and their legitimacy is weakened.

As is well known, tension and conflict are a sign of health in a system that thrives on its own contradictions, but the situation changes when its main constituents overgrow like cancerous cells.

A century ago, capitalism experienced such a long crisis, of which the "1929 crisis" was but the climax, and capitalism only got out of it after 1945. Going back over that period will help understand ours.

§ 2: A European Civil War

At the end of the nineteenth century, capitalism as it existed was no longer viable, on both sides of the capital-labour "couple": the productive forces of industry were too big to be managed by private owners, and the worker movement too powerful to be persistently denied a social and political role. Capitalism met the issue in a variety of ways. It did not turn "socialist" but it socialised itself, which took decades and included resistance, backlash, and outright reaction. (Fascism was one of them, a forced top-down national socialisation, as Stalinism was in a different way.) The evolution started with English trade unionism in the late nineteenth century and culminated in the post-1945 consumer society.

Reaching that stage took no less than a European civil war.

The conflicts of 1914–18 and 1939–45 were much more than interstate conflicts, and their paroxysmal violence was not only caused by the extermination capacity of industry. The political and military hubris unleashed by World War II remains a mystery if we neglect the 1920s and '30s confrontation between a restless militant working class, and a bourgeoisie wavering between repression and integration, combining both without opting for the one or the other. Imperial Germany and then Weimar were perfect examples of this situation, but so were Britain where the bourgeois waged a class war in the 1920s, especially against the miners, and the United States, where unionisation was de facto made impossible for millions of unskilled workers.

In 1914–18, mutual slaughter came close to a self-destruction of the belligerents, at least until U.S. intervention in 1917. Military *illimitation* illustrated the explosive power of the contradiction of a system dedicated to eliminate the remnants of the past, while trying to reunite in the trenches the classes of each country. And 1918 hardly solved anything. The most advanced country, the United States, exported its capital to Europe at the same time as it withdrew from the continent politically. Four outdated empires crumbled, and parliamentary democracy made headway but lacked the means to act as a social mediator. The two structuring classes of modern society remained stuck in a deadlock.

The 1917–39 period saw the breakdown of the international economy born at the end of the nineteenth century (the "first globalisation"). It was a time of dislocation, of nationalist upsurge, of conflicts between and within States, with the creation of new nation-states without real "national" basis, for lack of a domestic market that could have helped create a people's unity. (Two of them, Czechoslovakia and Yugoslavia, would break up at the time of the "second globalisation.") The mutual dependence of national economies on the world market is essential to capitalism (even the USSR was never totally walled-in), but this process is achieved with a succession and combination of openness (liberalism) and closure (Nazism and Stalinism). Amid these fault lines, the 1929 crisis added more class collision.

In Germany, it was not the huge unemployment rate that caused the rise of the Nazis: it was the German situation as a whole since 1918. The 1929 crash accelerated the ascension of Hitler by aggravating the political factors that had undermined Weimar since 1918. From 1930, the crash facilitated the advent of an authoritarian State, which ruled by government-decrees that deprived parliament of real power. It reduced the reformist capacity of the SPD and Centrum to next to nothing, marginalised the KPD even more, and increased the discrepancy between a democratic façade and a reactionary drift to the past, illustrated by the spread of *völkisch* nostalgia which conveyed a growing nationalist-racist mood and culture. (Unfortunately, idealists like Ernst Bloch were better equipped to understand this time-warp—when the past overlapped the present—than most materialists captive of a linear vision of history.)[2] The year 1929 finally signified the disunity of Germany and called for political forces able to reunite the country (the classes) through violence. Fortunes were ruined and beliefs as well. A political vacuum had to be filled, and it was not be done peacefully. Up to 1929, "conservative revolution" remained a contradiction in words: in the 1930s, the oxymoron became reality. As it militarised Germany, Nazism reforged a forced people's community closed in on the German race.[3]

Nazi warfare was a head-on pursuit in an all-or-nothing fight, involving planned genocide and implying the final self-immolation of the country: the regime sacrificed German unity rather than yield to clearly superior enemies. When the Nazis engaged in military competition with three great powers at the same time, this was absurd from a pragmatic point of view, yet consistent with the Nazi rise to power and the logic of the regime. This was no Clausewitz-style war aiming to achieve a decisive superiority and stopping when that goal was reached: for Hitler, annihilating the Jews and enslaving the Poles and the Russians were a priority.

In both world conflagrations, Germany stood at the epicentre, with at its heart a heavy industry constricted by a geopolitical framework that prevented it from exporting as much as its productive power required.

Various authors have suggested the idea of a "European civil war" from 1917 to 1945, but arch-conservatives, such as Ernst Nolte, best emphasised the *class* undercurrent of that period because of their "class reaction" and political bias.[4]

Whatever we think of the Russian revolution and its demise, the Bolsheviks' seizure of power was a death threat to the bourgeoisie worldwide. It is impossible to understand Mussolini and Hitler if we forget the fear (combining facts and fantasy) of the working class among the bourgeois, a fear shared by a large part of the petit-bourgeois.

Although the working class never seriously tried to overthrow bourgeois rule in Western Europe after 1918, what mattered was that unions and socialist parties were perceived as a challenge to be met. Fascism differed from the previous variants of reaction throughout the nineteenth century: it had roots in the industrial world, it drew in crowds, and it praised technique as much as it eulogised tradition, in that sense it partook of modernity. Against fascism, Roosevelt and the Popular Fronts reunited the worker movement and those bourgeois ready to let labour play its part politically alongside capital. In that contest, the bureaucratised worker movement led by Stalinism was both an ally and a rival of the Western bourgeoisies. It was therefore logical that national resistance against German occupation should often take on an antibourgeois look and discourse against traditional elites associated with fascism, in Yugoslavia, in Greece, and in Italy where patriotic war, civil war, and class war mingled against the *Nazifascist* enemy.

In 1939–45, instead of a proletariat v. bourgeoisie fight, but as a by-product of that previously inconclusive fight, three forms of capitalism confronted each other: the Russian bureaucratic statist version temporarily allied to the Anglo-Saxon liberal variant, against the German (and to a lesser extent Japanese) attempt to create self-sufficient empires.

After 1945, in Western Europe and Japan, parliamentarianism and the constitutional State finally fulfilled their function: to get a "people" together as a nation that integrated the labouring class. In 1943, a Tory politician, Quintin Hogg, said about the English workers: "We must give them reforms or they will give us revolution." The phrase was excessive, yet meaningful.

The year 1945 was to be different from 1918. At the end of World War I, the most powerful capitalist country stepped aside from European politics: the United States refused to be part of the League of Nations and showed little interest in the rise of Nazi Germany. While Roosevelt was busy with the New Deal, he hardly cared about the war in Spain. In 1945, the two major powers, the United States and USSR, did not just rule their own countries: each had the ability and the project to extend its domination over other parts of the world. Likewise, the bourgeois were not content with having the upper hand over the workers: the ruling class organised the capital-labour relation in such a way as to consolidate and perpetuate it.

§ 3: How Capitalism Globalised Its Crisis of the 1960s and '70s

The post-1945 "social peace" was limited to a few dominant countries, and even there "the affluent worker" was a myth.[5] Still, Western Europe developed various forms of the welfare state to pacify the toiling masses Quintin Hogg was worried about, and heavily indebted governments (backed by U.S. and Canadian credit) managed to produce the funding. An unspoken bargain was struck.

In the final decades of the twentieth century, worker pressure destabilised this consolidation. Much is known about a crisis that started forty years ago. We will only make two points. The bourgeois managed to quell worker unrest in the 1960s and '70s but (a) did not address the real issue, and (b) the way this "victory" was won and its aftermath have led to more social unbalance. This section analyses point (a) while the following paragraphs deal with point (b).

In the early 1970s, capitalist production was running into its inevitable periodic predicament: overaccumulation creates a mass of value so large that capital is unable to valorise it at the same rate as before. The all-too-visible forms of overcapacity and overproduction, not to mention the State "fiscal crisis," revealed profit deceleration.[6]

Business reengineering and *globalisation* were supposed to have remedied that.

As the word suggests, globalisation is perceived of as the creation of an open planetary market where investment, goods, and people could (or should) freely move as they please.

This is deceptive.

Firstly, monopolies and oligopolies have not put an end to State rule, which is in fact getting stronger in terms of law and order, and protectionism is not over.

Secondly, what is the bottom line of globalisation?

Downsizing, casualisation, substitution of individual contract for collective bargaining, outsourcing of manufacturing from one continent to another, promotion of the service sector at the expense of industry ... All the 1980s and '90s "restructuring" was based on one privileged factor: *the systematic lowering of labour costs.*

Cutting down wages is a bourgeois constant. "The innermost secret soul of English capitalism [is] the forcing down of English wages to the level of the French and the Dutch. . . . Today, thanks to the competition on the world-market . . . we have advanced much further." Marx quotes an English MP saying: "If China should become a great manufacturing country, I do not see how the manufacturing population of Europe could sustain the contest without descending to the level of their competitors." Marx concludes: "The wished-for goal of English capital is no longer Continental wages but Chinese." (*Capital*, vol. I, chap. 24, § 4)

Wages, however, though the most important variable in capitalism, are not the only one.

A remedy can prove worse than the cure.

Productivity gains were high again in the 1990s, especially in the United States, thanks to computerisation, the elimination of smokestack industries, and investment in low-labour-cost manufacturing in Asia. But however much computers and containers help compress and transfer labour, they only patch up the causes of profit decline. All the critical features of the '70s are still here forty years later, masked by the profits reaped by a minority of firms and by the windfall profits in the finance sector.

The current huge technical changes, particularly the computerisation of production and daily life, are misunderstood as a third "technological revolution" of comparable magnitude as those brought about by the steam engine in the early nineteenth century, and by electricity and the internal combustion engine in the late nineteenth–early twentieth. This is forgetting that productive forces are not mere technical tools. By themselves, petrol and chemistry would not have been enough to generate an industrial expansion between 1870 and 1914, and Taylorism-Fordism was a lot more than the conveyor belt.

The *social* dilemma of the interwar period (intensive accumulation without mass consumption) had been resolved in the post-1945 boom: intensive accumulation with mass consumption by transforming part of productivity gains into higher wages. In the aftermath of World War II, the United States would export goods that differed from those then known in Europe, manufactured by another type of management, and harbingers of an innovative lifestyle. On the contrary, in the late twentieth century, the Asian *tigers* and *dragons*, "New Industrial countries" as they were called, and now China, all too quickly labelled "the workshop of the world," make the most of existing techniques and manufacture the *same* objects as those made in the West, albeit at a lower cost. As supply exceeds demand, prices are pressed down . . . so are profits. The "long decline" that started in the mid-1970s has been compensated for but left unsolved. A new accumulation phase would imply more than technology, and require no less than the launching of new forms of production and labour, in other words a different regime of accumulation and a different mode of regulation. On the contrary, emerging economies rely on a *neo-Taylorism without Fordism*.[7]

The bourgeoisie has tried once more to short-circuit its partner-opponent by a roundabout technological fix, this time by a leap forward in MTC (Means of Transport and Communication): this is as successful as dosed-up growth can last.

Moreover, Chinese economy is not self-centred and at present no indicators show that it will cease being over-dependent on exports.

Besides, as it is transferred from the old industrial metropolises to Asia, labour gets organised, presses demands, and wage rises in China start forcing companies to invest in countries with a supposedly more docile workforce.

Globalising a problem is not enough to solve it. Internal production costs, as well as external and social costs (to remedy environmental damage), cannot be made up for by in-firm productivity gains, especially in countries which have opted for a service economy. The profitability revolution formerly experienced in agriculture and industry will never be on the same scale in the service sector: some of it is ideal for standardisation (telecommunications), some is not (health care).

There is no need to dwell on the fact that since 2008, the ruling classes have treated the crisis by means that perpetuate it. Lowering labour income for the sake of reducing companies' and governments' deficit, and injecting more cash into banks, will not address the basic issue: insufficient value creation and investment, which no expanding trade can compensate, particularly an expansion souped-up by credit. The bourgeoisie is going the opposite way of what helped come out of the Great Depression: demand support, public regulation, long-term investment.

So, if capitalism did make a fresh start at the end of the twentieth century, its victory was not what it seemed. The current crisis reveals that the 1980s and '90s boom did not overcome the 1970s predicament: overcapacity, overproduction, overaccumulation, declining profitability. The worldwide growth of the last thirty years is undeniable and unsound. Its success is based on causes that contradict the system's logic: capitalism cannot durably treat labour only as a cost to be reduced at all costs, prioritise the financial sector, live on debt, or extend the *American way of life* on all continents. Each Earthling, or even a couple of billion, will not possess a car, pool, and watered lawn.

§ 4: Neoliberalism Fallacy

While each of us is personally encouraged to live on credit, States are increasingly supposed to be run on the "prudent-person" principle of responsible management: "Let's not spend more public money than we have."

In fact, late-twentieth-century neoliberalism had little in common with nineteenth-century liberalism, when the bourgeois used to cut down on public expenditure, arguing that those sums would deplete their own hard-earned money and decrease investment. The role of the State and its budget were to be kept to a minimum.

This is not at all what Thatcher and Reagan initiated. When they increased public spending by debt financing, it did not help resolve the *fiscal crisis of the State*, nor was it that policy's goal: its dual purpose was to reduce the tax levy on companies and to reduce labour ability to put pressure on profits. Privatising and deregulating industry and banking (a process inaugurated in the United States by Jimmy Carter and continued by Bill Clinton after 1993) aimed to shatter the institutional framework which provided labour with means to defend itself (the famous "Fordist compromise"). Neoliberalism was doing away with mediations that gave a little individual and collective protection from market forces.

This had to occur at the core of the system: manufacturing, transport, and energy, namely sectors which were (and still are) vital and where worker organisation and unrest were the greatest. So the attack naturally targeted large factory and steel workers, miners, dockers, air traffic controllers, etc. As those key sectors were defeated, finance took the opportunity to push for its own interest at the expense of industry: this was a side effect of the evolution, not its cause.

The rise of Asia was another consequence of labour defeat. U.S., European, and Japanese bourgeois started manufacturing products in Asia or Latin America, then opened their markets to Chinese imports, only *after* having crushed worker militancy in their own countries.

§ 5: Wages, Price, and Profit

A Niagara of articles has been written to explain how the bourgeois (usually called the rich) have been stealing from the poor for the last decades. Quite true, but the relevant question is whether after 1980 the bourgeois counterattack on labour was successful . . . or too much so. Systematic negation of the role of labour (i.e., systematic downsizing manpower and cutting down labour costs) brings profits in the short term but proves detrimental in the long run. Global growth figures of world trade and production in the last thirty years obscure the essential: there are still not enough profits to go round. *Faster* capital circulation does not necessarily coincide with *better profits*. In 2004, a number of French companies increased their yearly profits by 55 percent, mainly because they freed themselves of their *own* less rewarding sectors. The question is how far insufficient profitability can be compensated by a strategy that benefits a minority entrenched in strategic *niches* (the expanding high-tech business, companies with strong links to public spending, and last but not least finance). There is nothing new here. What was called the *mixed economy* or *State monopoly capitalism* in the 1950–80 period also relied on a constant transfer of money from business as a whole to a happy few companies.[8] But the running of such a system implied a modicum of dynamism: the most powerful firms would have been unable to take more than their share of profits if overall profitability had been lacking.

Capitalism is not simply an accumulation of money at one pole (capital) and an outright lowering of costs on the other (labour). And even less so an accumulation of speculative windfall profits made at the expense of the "real" economy, that is, companies that make and sell items (be they mobile phones or online bought films). Capitalism cannot be just *money sold for money*.

From the mid-nineteenth century onward, capital has always had to take labour into account, even under Stalin and Hitler.[9] If there is one lesson to be learned from Keynes, it is that labour is both a cost *and an investment*.

There is a limit to what capitalism can exclude without reaching a highly critical stage: in a world where the economy and work reign, the continuity and stability of the existing social order depends on its ability to put at least a fair amount of proletarians to productive work.

Productive in more than one sense: productive of value for companies to accumulate and invest; productive of wealth for the ruling classes and of money for taxes; productive of what is needed for the upkeep and reproduction of the dispossessed as a distinct group and a pool of potential labour; productive of the necessary maintenance of what remains of other classes; and productive of "meaning," of collective ideas, images, and myths capable of getting classes together and taking them along toward some common goal: a society, and this applies to capitalist society as well, is not an accumulation of passive workers and atomised consumers.

The nexus here is how much capital's treatment of labour affects the reproduction of society. The renewal of the labour force has to be global, both social and political.

On the contrary, reengineering has been functioning since the 1980s as if labour was open to ruthless exploitation. Manpower looks inexhaustible (bosses can always replace insubordinate or aging proletarians with fresh ones), yet it is not.

In nineteenth-century European factories (as in many factories in the emerging countries today), the bourgeois would exploit workers until they wore out. This brought in lots of profits for years, but when the army called up millions of adult males in 1914, the military realised that the lower classes were plagued by malnutrition, morbidity, rickets, and disability. It is fine for the individual boss to care only about the value produced by his company. Bosses as a class have to take into account the *reproduction* of the labouring class. Misery and profit do not always get on well: labour is often more productive when he is better paid, housed, fed, kept in good health, and even treated with a modicum of respect.

Socially, "rich" countries have abandoned their poorest 20 percent to their dismal fate. The relative part of wage-labour in national income has gone down (sometimes by 10 percent) in the United States and in most old industrial countries. Millions of young adults live in poverty, and there are more and more *working poor* and *new poor*, blue collar and petty office workers (60 percent of the working population in France) are being levelled down, yet upper-class victory has its price. The drive to ultraproductivity causes *work stress*, loss of working hours and other expenses, the burden of which ultimately weighs on collective capital. Likewise, cutting down the "social" wage is short-sighted policy: money spent on education, health, and pension is an investment which benefits capital's cycle. Too much cost-cutting has brought in quick profits, but the incidental expenses of globalisation will have to be paid for.

The more and more unequal sharing of profits between capital and labour is one aspect of a lack of profitability, caused not by the greed of financiers (the bourgeois are no more or less greedy today than yesterday), but by the shortage of profits gained in industry and commerce. If one leaves the United States aside, "the world economy proves incapable of sustaining a demand that would keep its productive (and particularly) industrial capacities busy." This was the point made in 2005 by a French economist with no Marxist or leftist leanings, Jean-Luc Gréau.[10] He argued that the systematic worldwide lowering of labour costs is part of the problem, not the solution: "How do economists manage to publicly ignore the effects of wage deflation on the world situation? . . . Wage deflation means deflation of value creation."

The Walmartisation of North America is more than a symbol. With its cheaply *made in China* articles, temp work imposed on one third of its personnel, an average wage that would have been classified as a secondary income thirty years ago, and its de facto union bashing, Walmart's low-cost system is perfectly adapted (and contributes) to overall declining incomes. This is Keynesianism in reverse: low wages are the condition of low consumption. A society that needs "food banks" and has charity shops in every English town centre is ill suited for prosperous trade.

As mass consumption is now a cornerstone of capitalism, systematic downsizing and outsourcing finally lower the purchasing power of wage-earners and the unemployed. Far from being a mere fiction, money is *substantified* labour, and the relevance of money derives from the living labour that it represents. When labour is degraded, neither rich nor poor can endlessly buy on installment, and sooner or later the debt economy meets its limits. Underconsumption is an effect, not a cause, but it intensifies the crisis.

Politically, the bourgeoisie needs workers who work and who keep quiet when they are out of work. As long as wage-labour exists, there will never be enough work for everyone. But there has to be enough of it for society to remain stable, or at least manageable.

Capitalism's logic has never been to include everyone as a capitalist or wage-earner, nor to turn the whole planet into middle-class suburbia. Nevertheless, capital-labour relations necessitate some balance between development and underdevelopment, wealth and poverty, official and unofficial labour, job security and casual work, stability and flexibility. Otherwise, the privileged residents from suburbia will be afraid to go shopping downtown at the risk of being met by underclass gangs, muggers, or looters. Too many gated communities coexisting with too many slums make a socially explosive cocktail. A society cannot be pacified only by police.

In order to reproduce itself, capitalism must not only feed and house wage-workers but reproduce what constitutes their lives, family, education, health—the whole of daily life. The supposedly normal course of capitalism is far from peaceful, and social tensions in Turin, 2000, are different from Manchester, 1850: *food* riots are rarely to be seen in "rich" countries now, though millions of U.S. citizens have to eat on food stamps. Poverty and want change with the times. If contemporary daily life has been successfully turned into a succession of purchases (millions of people trade on eBay and similar sites), that does not prevent the repetition of riots in the old capitalist centres as in the new ones. Looting is not revolution, but when the poor take to the streets to go looting, as in London in 2011, it shows the market unleashes forces it cannot control.

When the bourgeois wonder how to bring back solvency not only to large masses but to whole countries, it is because the *wage relation* runs the risk of no longer adequately providing conditions for *social reproduction*.

§ 6: The Impossibility of Reducing Everything to Time

When driven to extremes, the permanent search for time-saving becomes counterproductive. Shortening time results in everything being treated short-time. In 1960, the success of the *American way of life* was proved by its ability to convince the motorist to buy a new car model every two years: fifty years later, our home computer recommends we update our software every other week. Built-in obsolescence conflicts with *sustainable* growth and *renewable* energy: the essence of time is that it can neither be stored nor renewed.

There comes a point where social pressures no longer drive the system forward but rather strain it. What previously made it strong—to separate, quantify, and circulate everything at maximum possible speed—turns against it.

Time is a contemporary obsession, at work, at home, in the street, everywhere. When companies try to produce and circulate everything in *real time*, what they are really aiming at is *zero* time. Modern individuals cannot bear to do only one thing at a time. A Martian visitor might think we manufacture and consume not so much objects as speed. Competition forces each firm to minimise labour costs, and each worker's contribution is to be counted in time—however debatable the resulting figure will be. Computers and experts are there to economise time, to absorb it, eventually to nullify it: "Time and space don't exist anymore," says your HP Photosmart printer software. Yet this never goes fast enough to make time profitable enough.

Capitalism always proves at its best in the short term, but nowadays it lacks some vision of the future and some public regulation that only work in long time frames.

§ 7: Shareholder Capitalism

The enterprise is central to capitalism. It provides the continuity of capital as an entity distinct from those who own it, manage it and work for it: it could replace them all with entirely new owners, managers, and workers, and still go on. Shareholders and managers are equally necessary.

What is now called "shareholder capitalism" follows a different logic. Letting the shareholders run the enterprise has given top priority to the dividend over the benefit. The need for the firm to bring in the maximum to the shareholders, even at the expense of the firm, contradicts the function of the entrepreneur as the agent of value accumulation. Too much profit given back to the work force will reduce profitability. But too much profit claimed by a nineteenth-century factory owner, or by a twenty-first-century pension fund, means a dysfunctional valorisation cycle. Capital does not exist to enrich the bourgeois at any cost or to enrich bourgeois fractions at the expense of the whole.

Kant's philosophical dove thought the air around its wings was an obstacle and believed it would fly better in a void. Likewise, capital's utopia is to free itself from blue-collar workers and just keep flexible intellectual labour, as if it could feed on itself and develop as a sum of value that had done away with the conditions that produced it. It's not enough for capital to picture itself liberated from labour: it also wants to break loose from matter (no factory, no goods, no stock or as little as possible, just a flow of value), and finally from money itself (no gold, no cash, only credit lines, figures on a screen, 0 and 1 digits). Freed from the constraints of space by relocation, capital dreams of becoming a mere movement through time. In fact, an engine with neither piston nor rod, with neither fuel nor operator, would no longer be an engine, but just the abstraction of motion, the principles of mechanics applied to a virtual machine. In that case, profits are virtual too. If time measuring and saving are certainly at the heart of the value cycle, valorisation is the transformation of human activity into something profitable, be it an X-rated film or a loaf of bread, but something that's eventually bought with a benefit for the seller and producer. Financiers exchange between themselves: they do not reproduce themselves. The wonders of capitalist incest turn out to be monsters.

The stock market is necessary for capitalism, which needs a meeting place between the enterprise and the investor, for title deeds to be compared and exchanged. Yet today's astounding groundswell in stock market valuation does not correspond to a mass issuing of shares sold to finance investments. Most of the issuing takes place within firms that buy back their own shares to push up their price (and take advantage of this overpricing to help them borrow more), or between firms, when one company buys another one. Nowadays, more money is spent repurchasing shares and paying out dividends than in issuing new shares. Because the inflow of money exceeds the possibilities of sufficient returns, firms buy themselves back, in order to increase a shareholding value unlinked to actual results. When a company buys back its own assets, it's tantamount to a "decapitalisation" (J.-L. Gréau): the company pays (often a lot) for its own capital and makes no fresh investment. The shareholders get richer without the company yet realising any profit.

Whereas private speculators and bankers can get out of the share market if they think it's in their best interest, pension funds and hedge funds live off that market and tend to maintain valorisations disconnected from the effective results of companies. This leads to a closed-circuit system that knows no other regulation but itself, with no guidelines that would compel it to rationalise itself before it reaches breaking point.

There's nothing absurd in a stock market valuation being nine hundred times the total of the annual profit of a firm (Yahoo in 2000), or sixty times (Google in 2006). Those figures signal the investors' logical behaviour in the face of truly outstanding achievements in a promising sector. What's wrong is to equate the capital of a firm with a valuation that only reflects the mutual trust of economic actors: that trust has only the rationality of reciprocal optimisms.

Ideologically, the bourgeois have won: media present the financial crisis as a *debt* problem (meaning: you and I are paid too much). In reality, what was unlikely in 1960 (a chain-reaction financial bankruptcy similar to the post-1929 one) because of corporate and State safeguards, has turned into a possibility. True, the State has more leeway, as when the Federal Reserve forced U.S. banks to bail out the hedge fund LTCM (total losses: $4.6 billion) in 1998. The shockwaves of the crisis of the "new" Asian industrial countries after 1997 were contained, as well as the breakdown of other fragile economies in Latin America, and later the "new economy" crash. The 2007–2008 "global crisis" has been survived. But will States be able to play this stabilising role if confronted with multiple bankruptcies? Globalisation opens up the possibility of a systemic crisis.

§ 8: A Class Out of Joint

When left to themselves, the bourgeois seek their own maximum profit, and follows their natural inclination to combine technical prowess with money grabbing. One of their recent favourite ways has been to promote the domination of interest-bearing capital over industrial and commercial capital.

Since the Industrial Revolution, hypertrophied finance has usually been a sign of capital overdrive. Low break-even point in manufacturing and trade spawns a tendency to seek higher capital efficiency in money circulation, which inevitably results in crude and sophisticated speculation. This works fine—as long as it lasts—for the happy few in Wall Street and the City, but it results in an imbalance between the various bourgeois strata.

There is a connection between labour's defeat at the end of the 1970s, and the shake-outs which have occurred in finance since. Financial freewheeling is one of capital's preferred methods of negating what creates it: labour. Credit means spending the money one does not have but hopes to get, for instance by turning the (expected) rise of one's house on the property market into an increased borrowing capacity. Money, however, is not endowed with an endless power of self-creation: it only makes the world go round in so far as it is crystallised labour. Financial crash is a reality check: between labour and capital, the cause-and-effect relation is not what the bourgeois would like to think. Labour sets capital (and money) into motion, not the other way round.

Speculation is a natural, and indeed indispensable feature of capitalism: overspeculation heralds financial storms.

As class struggle turned in favour of the bourgeois after 1980, they took maximum advantage of the situation, of course at the expense of the proletarians, but also with a power shift within the ruling class, and the rise of financial capitalists exacting two-figure profits when industrial profit rarely exceeds 3–4 percent per year in the long run. *Rent*, formerly surplus profits obtained by monopolising the access to resources or technologies, has tended to become the dominant form of bourgeois income: securitisation (transforming debt into commodities), derivative markets (literally selling and buying the future: insurance, options, risks, derived from existing assets), speculation on commodities, speculative bubbles (particularly on the property market), stock options, etc. Hi-tech and cybereconomy revive a *rentier class* Keynes wished to see euthanised in the interest of the system as a whole. Financial escalation and unprecedented money creation by banks are too well known for us to go into any detail here.

Some synergy must be found between financier and engineer, shareholder and manager. Share prices are not the only yardstick for deciding the optimum cost-benefit ratio. Financial products are as "real" as ironmongery, but only in so far as they are developed in parallel to manufactured and sold objects and services that are more than mere money flows.

All bourgeois share a common position as a class. It is the would-be reformers (often repentant intellectuals familiar with the corridors of power, like Joseph Stiglitz, policymaker in the World Bank and the Clinton administration) who theorise the "real" economy and differentiate true entrepreneurs from money-makers. The bourgeois are divided but stand as one against labour to defend their interlaced interests. There was no cohesion in the German ruling class in the 1920s, until it rallied behind Hitler. A lot will depend on whether financial, industrial, and commercial sectors will remain disunited or converge on a policy of reform.

§ 9: The Money God That Fails

When the worker struggles of the 1960s–70s were contained, unchecked capitalism acted as if it was free to capitalise everything, the air we breathe, the human genome, or the Rialto Bridge. Anything is liable to become an adjunct to value production or an object of commerce.

Though this trend to universal commoditisation is more proof of capital's omnipresence, capitalism cannot do with an *entirely* capitalised society: it needs institutions and norms that are subordinate to it, but it also needs them *not* to directly comply with the profit imperative. Schools are not supposed to add value to a capital. Civil servants are not businessmen. "Research and development" requires basic research. Accounting requires trustworthy figures. The same company which fiddles its own book expects to be provided with honest government statistics. Public services have to submit to capitalist standards yet retain a certain degree of autonomy.

If the limits of *Homo economicus* are now being debated, if Karl Polanyi and his critique (*The Great Transformation*, published in 1944) of the illusion of a self-regulating market become fashionable, it shows that even the liberals have to admit the necessity of restraining the grip of profit-making over society. Polanyi contended that the human propensity toward the market was historical, not natural: capitalism had *disembedded* the production of the means of existence from both social life and nature. No Marxist and certainly not a communist, Polanyi was not opposed to the existence of a market: his remedy to the autonomisation of the economy was to *reembed* productive activity within mutual links.

Written in the aftermath of the Great Depression, this critique coincided with a capitalist effort to regulate market forces. In the last decades, there has been a renewed interest in Polanyi's emphasis on "embeddedness": reformers would like the economy to be brought under social control, in order to create a sustainable relationship with nature.

Polanyi had a point: individualist money exchange erodes the social fabric. He only failed to see that we cannot expect capitalism to limit itself: the market always tends to overdevelop. As the liberals are right to point out, the advantages of capitalism come with its defects. In the colleges where *The Great Transformation* is taught, managers dream of tying teacher pay to students' performance on standardised tests. Polanyi was a naive believer in the self-critique of capitalism.

§ 10: Quantifying the Qualitative (When the Disease Becomes the Medicine)

How does a system based on universal measuring react to excess quantitativism? By quantifying quality. You can now do a PhD in Happiness Studies: Gross Domestic Product is fine when complemented by Gross National Happiness (GNH).

At a time when the West doubts its own values and looks to the East for soul food, it is not by chance that GNH originated in Bhutan, the first country where it was first officially used. The concept was not born out of pure tradition but was invented by the local rulers when Bhutan was going through a modernisation process—a code phrase for entering the capitalist age. GNH was to act as a bridge between mercantile pressures and the prevailing Buddhist mind-set, and to provide Bhutanese society with an ideology presenting wage-labour and a money economy as suited to the well-being of people. Similar surveys followed in "modern" countries, and opinion polls now collect data on well-being.[11]

It is a well-known sociological "law" that in a survey the questions determine the answers: the sophisticated indicators used in interviews to measure the population's well-being served to hammer into Bhutanese heads the idea that Bhutan's evolution was good for them.

GNH is as manipulative as GDP but also equally deceptive for its users, be they experts or the rulers that pay the experts. While it claims to be a guide to proper planning for the future, and to be taking into account factors that are not strictly economic, GNH works with the same logic as value: it puts everything together, from the water table to school attendance, and synthesises it (or pretends to) in order to reach figures and graphs that reduce reality to common features. Applying econometrics to daily life cannot compensate for the lack of a general vision that the present competing world of States and companies is by its nature incapable of achieving, as everybody actually knows. It is an open secret that GNH compilations scarcely help upgrade sustainable development, cultural integrity, ecosystem conservation, and good governance. But never mind. As GNH fails to quantify well-being and happiness, new constructs see the light of day, like the Genuine Progress Indicator. As mental health does not suffice, emotional health is now deemed metrically measurable. When factual data prove inadequate, specialists compile memories. When *wellness* falls short of required norms, a long list of various wellnesses is made up, and new papers are written.

The *figure* society is also a *report* society. In 2001, the United Nations launched a Millennium Ecosystem Assessment project to evaluate the financial costs of ecosystem losses. Its estimate for 1982–2002 was $180,000 billion. The figure has been contested, which requires more MEA studies. Productivism may be discredited in manufacturing, not in research.

Happiness teachers are the contemporary lay preachers that patch up the inadequacies and monstrosities of present times. It is quite natural that Happiness research should obey the reductionist, figure-obsessed logic that prevails in intellectual and political life, or in education, where schoolchildren are assessed by box-ticking: we are all benchmarked now. Tellingly, this is not what critics object to. They charge that governments define GNH as it suits them: isn't that the case with all statistics? They deplore the unscientific criteria: how could well-being fit in with any objective standard? Only a scientist mind can regard happiness as an object of science, or emotion as an analogue to economic progress. They bemoan the national bias, but it was inevitable that Bhutan should find comfort in its own version of GNH. A twenty-first-century U.S. GNH would validate the *American way of life* as the United States likes to picture itself *now*, a multicultural, eco-conscious, minority-friendly society, certainly not as it was in 1950.

GNH is a product of a time when a GDP-led world is in crisis, and it deals *ideologically* with its crisis. Zen wisdom goes well with GNH.

§ 11: Forbidden Planet?

A system bent on treating labour as an infinitely exploitable asset acts the same toward nature. As early as the 1950s and '60s, farsighted observers warned about ecological risks.[12] Yet, as a whole, post-1980 growth has meant more production, more energy (including nuclear energy) consumption, and more planned obsolescence.

A capitalist contradiction has become more visible and more acute than a century ago: if this mode of production is bound to commoditise everything, this process includes its environment ("nature"), which can never be completely turned into commodities. It is economically sound for a fridge or a video-on-demand to be indefinitely interchangeable and renewable. The same logic does not apply to trees, fish, water, or fossil fuels. It is going to be harder to do something about CO_2 than it was in the 1930s to remedy the damage done by the Dust Bowl. Even if the United States benefits from shale oil and shale gas (which now generates a highly profitable fracking boom), for most countries the cost of fossil energy will continue to rise and become increasingly uneconomical, which does not mean that this will block the system: there is always a way out of a severe profitability dilemma, a calamitous way.

Capitalism must find some balance between itself and what it feeds on, with its social as well as natural environment: "nature" is one of those indispensable not-to-be-fully-capitalised elements.

What is involved here is first the wage versus profit issue, but also everything it implies. Company, wage-labour, and commodity are indeed the heart of the system, but that heart only beats by pumping what fuels it, humankind and first of all labour power, and also nature.

One does not have to be an ecological catastrophist to realise the contrast between the beginning of the twenty-first century and the situation in 1850 or 1920. A huge difference with the 1914–45 crisis is that accumulation now meets ecological limits as well as social ones: overexploitation of fossil fuels, overurbanisation, overuse of water, climate risks . . . combine so that the mode of production uses up its natural capital, while the decline of Keynesianism deprives the State of its former regulating capacities.

When private market forces are no longer checked by public counterpower, capital's inherent limitation is given free rein. Deregulation, privatisation, and commercialisation have contributed to deplete natural conditions that cannot be infinitely renewed. In fifty years, chemistry and agribusiness have multiplied by four or five the yield of wheat-growing land . . . providing the farmer inputs ten calories to get an output of one. The day capital has to factor in all the elements necessary to production, overexploitation will start becoming economically unprofitable.

Up to now, business could regard energy inputs, raw materials and environment as expendable sources of wealth that were taken for granted. As long as the cost of water pollution by the aluminium factory for the rest of society would not be paid for by either the producers or buyers, business could ignore it. Such a "negative externality" must now be integrated into production costs: this, capital finds difficult to do, and so far there has been less action than talk, with "systems thinking" and "systemic approach" becoming buzzwords. "De-growth," "un-growth," or "zero growth" are incompatible with a system that still relies on mass manufacturing and buying of big (cars) or small (e-readers) items, planned obsolescence, and huge coal-fired or nuclear power stations. The smartphone is as much productivist as the Cadillac car.

Ecology is now part of ruling class ideology. It has even given birth to a new popular genre: doomsaying, which in true religious fashion thrives on fear and guilt: the fault lies in human acquisitiveness, in our ingrained materialistic foolish hedonism.

Yet the world is not determined by the opposition between man and nature, between technique and nature, between a destructive megamachine and the continuation of life. The biosphere is indeed one of the limits against which capitalism collides, but the connection between the human species and the biosphere is mediated by social relations. The "nature" we are talking about is not external to the present mode of production: raw materials and energy are part of the framework whereby labour produces capital.

Electricity, for instance, perfectly suits capitalism: it exists as a mere flow that is not easy to store, and therefore must keep on circulating. If its production costs happen to exceed its benefit, what can business do except pass on the buck to the State, but where does public money come from? We are faced with the paradox of an amazingly mobile and adaptable system that has gradually built itself on an increasingly nonreproducible material basis.

Human, social, and natural ability to adapt, for better or worse, are certainly larger than we think. Soon we might have to get used to living in a highly dangerous environment. The Japanese start to wonder what is worse for a child: to play in an irradiated playground environment or be banned from outdoor playing? Nuclear power creates a situation when capitalist investment could stop being profitable. For its own reproduction, a social system feeds on (human and natural) energy and raw materials. If a system spends more resources on preserving its environmental conditions than it gets out of them, if the social input exceeds the social output, society breaks down.

As present society is unable to address the issue on anything like the scale necessary, two options combine: mild accommodation, and playing the *sorcerer's apprentice*. Science, business, and government are currently cooking up imaginative and (allegedly) profitable geoengineering solutions such as removing carbon dioxide from the atmosphere and depositing it elsewhere (like "advanced" countries shipping their industrial toxic waste to Africa), managing solar radiation to cool the planet by reflecting radiation into space, fertilising oceans with iron, and cloud brightening. If climate goes wrong, let's have weather control, and if industry puts the environment at risk, let's change nature.[13]

Dodging the obstacle by the same means that creates it: one wonders which is worse, the failure or success of such science-fictional projects.

§ 12: No Capitalist Self-Reform

There is no shortage of lucid perceptive minds in capitalism. Indeed, some of its early theoreticians suggested restraint (A. Smith) or reforms (Sismondi).[14] Nevertheless, such moderating influence fell on deaf ears, unless it was backed by mass action, strike, riot, Chartism, the Paris Commune, fear of revolution, or in the United States the violence narrated by Louis Adamic's *Dynamite* (1931). It always takes more than books and speeches for a class to realise where its long-term interest lies.

Only organised labour forced doses of regulation upon reluctant bourgeois: no New Deal without the sit-down strikes.

On the contrary, in the ebb of struggles, freewheeling capitalism acts as if it could make the most money out of anything.

Today, the more data are collected, the more sophisticated software and applied maths become (*high-frequency trading*), the less self-control there seems to be. A case in point is the reluctance to separate investment from commercial banking, as compared to the scope of the Glass-Steagall Act in 1933. Instead, the rulers look for more control over work and over the people. Neoliberalism never minds government when government deals with law and order, and it is quite compatible with bureaucracy. Laws, regulations, guidelines, protocols, and codes of ethics have proliferated with the computerised standardisation of every domain from medical care to education or the stock exchange. The *precautionary principle* is hyped by the same society that keeps playing with fire (nuclear risk being just one example). Potentially unhealthy industrialised food is served by glove-wearing shop assistants. The consensus is that the more information we read on packets or on the web, the safer we are. The "Knowing Is Doing" fallacy is typical of a world in disarray.

Self-control has never been capitalism's strong point. The bourgeois excels in making use of human and natural resources to produce and accumulate but, despite thousands of think tanks, he is unable to think of capitalism as a totality because it is *not his business*, literally. When a company invests in a factory or a mine, the managers make the most of workforce, raw materials, and technology, and only take care of the rest (occupational accidents, toxic waste, water pollution, etc.) if and when they come under pressure from the work force, law, local authority or whistleblowers. Bourgeois priority is to increase the productivity of labour and capital: that is what they are bourgeois for and they prove good at it. Long-term and "holistic" thinking come second.

Paradoxically, the abundance of reform "road maps" is a sign of procrastination. Most schemes conform to the current tendency of increased individualisation. Whenever the possibility of higher direct or social wage is raised, it is usually conditioned on the wage-labourer *personally* submitting to overtime, compulsory retraining, a private insurance policy, etc. This neglects that a social compact is only viable if it is collectively entered into and respected: in other words, collective bargaining. Yet the bourgeoisie persists in treating society as a combination of single atoms free to associate or stay apart. Historical replies to social questions cannot be individual.

Capitalism's challenge nowadays is to make labour more profitable and also to restore a working balance between accumulation and natural conditions. The ruling classes are evading both issues.

European politics is a clear illustration of this. The rush to unity almost immediately followed the proletarian defeat of the 1970s. At the same time as China was busy accumulating dollars thanks to the U.S. trade deficit, the euro was born. This single currency was groundless: it did not come out of any socioeconomic, let alone political, coherence. What is sometimes called the biggest single world market is nothing more: the European Union is a five-hundred-million-strong market devoid of common purpose and political leadership. Nation-building took centuries in Europe. State is now declared outmoded, whereas trade is regarded as a pacifier, equaliser and unifier. A single currency has been imposed upon unequal, rival, and *still national* economies, as if Greece could quietly coexist with Germany (two-thirds of the German trade surplus comes from the euro-zone), while the European budget is a trifling amount compared to the U.S. federal budget. This is tantamount to diluting the social question by extending it over a larger and larger geographic area.

§ 13: Deadlock

The proletarians are not just victims of capitalist contradictions: their resistance deepens these contradictions. Chinese workers put forward wage claims. Thousands of miles away, Accor hotel cleaners fight for better working conditions. Even when defeated, and it often is, labour unrest aggravates the crisis, and contributes to a social stalemate in which up to now all classes take part, as between the two world wars.

Unlike the 1930s, however, no New Deal is in sight. Far-reaching reform is impossible without a large deep social movement: deprived of mass pressure on the shop floor and in the street, reformers remain powerless.

In the mid-twentieth century, in spite and because of proletarian defeats, the labour/capital confrontation finally entailed an adjustment of the exploitation of labour and began to regulate itself, with the "capital + labour + State" association.

Today, opposed classes counteract each other without any reformist nor (yet) revolutionary prospect. Up to now, capital disrupts and breaks apart labour far more than labour practically challenges its own reality. As we will see in the next chapter, few acts could qualify as *anti-work* or *anti-proletarian*.

Though the past is never reenacted, the interwar period offered a not too dissimilar picture, with the bourgeoisie proving unable to reform capitalism and the working class unable to overthrow it, until political and military violence unblocked the historical evolution.

As recalled in § 2, three forms of capitalism coexisted and fought in the 1930s and '40s: a "market" type led by the United States and Britain; a "State bureaucratic" type in the USSR; and a German very different but also State-managed type, where under Nazi rule the bourgeois kept their property and wealth but lost political leadership.

We now know what happened in 1945 and later in 1989, but in 1930 or 1950 very few (bourgeois or revolutionaries) were able to tell how it would all unfold. It is easy to explain today why the variant most adequate to the inner nature of capitalism would come out as the winner, but the other variants proved fairly resilient, to say the least. The vagaries of twentieth-century class struggle brought the unexpected: though they were indeed capitalist (and it was essential for radical critique to be clear on that issue, as it still is now), Stalinism and Nazism did not fit well with capitalism as communist theory *was able to understand it at the time*.

Because the State absorbs and concentrates society's potential violence, intra- and inter-State contradictions, far from being neutralised, generate multiple tensions and conflicts, including those now called ethnic. Contemporary globalisation inevitably comes with the prospects of war. The 1914–45 era reminds us that in the absence of revolution, disorder and cataclysm can throw a social system into turmoil without terminating it.

§ 14: No "Creative Destruction" . . . Yet

All the components of the crisis we have summed up refer to the degree of exploitation, to the relation between the two classes that structure the modern world.

When labour pressure is unable to moderate private capital and influence public policy, the tendency is for wages to go down, consumption to rely on instalment buying, finance to dominate industry, privatisation to develop at the expense of public services, money to colonise society, the market to evade regulation and short-termism to prevail over long-term investment and planning. At the end of the nineteenth century and then after the 1917–45 European civil war, worker unrest, in spite of its nonrevolutionary character, threatened profits until it forced the bourgeois into better-adapted forms of exploitation. Labour countervailing action periodically drives capital forward and both softens and *worsens* its domination: "taming" capital reinforces it.

The transition from Keynesian-Fordist *national* compromise to *globalised* unbridled bourgeois rule resulted from a shift in the social balance of power. After 1945, the business-union-State settlement depended on the ability of labour to impose some form of deal. The 1960s–70s struggles put an end to give and take. The ruling class won.

Today's class struggle in the West combines labour resistance and bourgeois refusal to give up even a portion of its vested interests. The interlocking of the two forces results in a stalemate than cannot go on forever.

Capital has acted as if it could disintegrate labour, or even *obliterate* it, as bluntly put by professor Michael Hammer in 1990, whereas labour is the stuff capital is made of. It is sound capitalist strategy to lower the cost of labour in Denver by having local workers buy cheaper imported goods. This is what Britain did in 1846 with the repeal of Corn Laws that limited food imports: cheaper bread reduced labour's *cost of life*, hence wages. But when U.S. capital gives Denver labour the strictest minimum pay to buy mainly made in China goods, there is a flaw: what will be manufactured in Denver, and what to do with the local proles? Not everyone has the chance to become a computer specialist, nor the ability to live on diminishing social benefits: will work in the future be (in the best of cases) casual, or (more likely) a succession of menial odd jobs and periods on the dole? Bourgeois answer is *yes*: there will remain a lot of unemployed and working poor in Denver for quite a while, but it does not matter because they can still eat junk food and afford Asian-manufactured cell phones. It is logical, but the logic is warped.

Prioritising global over local, uncoupling the wage-worker income from the society and the market where he lives, would be feasible if labour was as flexible, fluid, separable, and expandable as figures, indeed . . . as *money*, which is transferable, interchangeable, and dispensed with at will. And this precisely is the capitalist dream. The present condition of the world and the current crisis prove how strong this utopia is, and how wrong: virtuality is a fallacy. The "real" economy may not be as tangible as it seems, but it has a degree of reality that the financial universe is lacking. One can play with money, "liquefy" banks, and launch credit lines at will for years. On the contrary, labour is neither virtual nor virtualisable.

Capitalism never overcomes its contradictions: it shifts them, adapts them to its logic while adapting itself to them.

"Capitalist production seeks continually to overcome these immanent barriers, but overcomes them only by means which again place these barriers in its way and on a more formidable scale." (*Capital*, Vol. 3, chap. 15)

Capitalism is based on its ability to provide wage-labour with means of existence. It can keep going with billions of people starving, as long as the *core*—value production—perpetuates itself on a constantly enlarged scale (as required by competitive dynamics: today Shanghai is part of the *centre* of the system as much as Berlin). Manchester was prosperous while "the bones of cotton-weavers [were] bleaching the plains of India," as the governor general of India wrote in 1834. Utmost misery is no big news.

The bourgeois problem is twofold:

(a) The core itself is in deep trouble. A social system can make do with starving masses, as long as its heart provides sufficient pump action: capitalist "heart" is a value pump, and for forty years the pump has not been delivering enough, however much profit is made by a minority of firms, and however much money is created and circulated.

(b) The heart of the matter is not the whole matter. Capitalism as it exists in the United States, Europe, China, and beyond cannot go on in an eruptive, explosive world. Though eruption does not mean revolution (to give just one example, social violence in Bangladesh is as much related to religion as to class), but business needs a minimum of law and order as well as political stability.

We are not talking about countries or parts of the world (North/South, the West/Asia), but about "unequal development" within nearly every country. The ruling classes are not particularly worried about what goes on in a backwater Bolivian province, a miserable London estate, or a deprived Islamabad district, and just deal with it by appropriate doses of police beatings and public relief. A very different situation arises when Bolivian villagers, rebellious English youths, or rioting urban Pakistanis create unmanageable political confusion, disturb the flow of national capital, disrupt world trade, and indirectly cause war and geopolitical chaos. Class struggle strictly speaking (viz. merely involving bourgeois v. proletarians) is not the only factor that sets capitalism off course.

Capitalism is based on conditions that must be reproduced *as a whole*: labour first, also everything that holds society together, not forgetting its natural bases. "Crisis of civilisation" occurs when the social system only achieves this through violent tremors and shocks, which eventually drive it to a new threshold of contradiction management.

In our time, if capitalism finds a way out of the crisis, recovery will not be soft and irenic. Social earthquakes, political realignments, war, impoverishment will come together with consumer individualism in the shadow of a domineering State, in a mixture of modernity and archaism, permissiveness and religious fundamentalism, autonomy and surveillance, moral disorder and order, democracy and dictatorship. The nanny State and militarised police go hand in glove. In the emblematic capitalist country, New Orleans after Katrina in 2005 provided us with glimpses of a possible future: infrastructure breakdown, overburdened public services, effective but insufficient grass-roots self-help, law and order restored by armoured vehicles.

Defining a crisis is not telling how it will be settled. No European or North American country is now approaching the point where class disunity, political confrontation, ruin of the State and loss of control on the part of the ruling class would prevent the fundamental social relation—capital/labour—from operating, but conditions are building up to create such a situation.

One thing is certain. The historical context calls for an even much deeper response than in the 1930s, and no solution is on the way, no "creative destruction," to use a phrase coined by Schumpeter in the middle of a world war.

§ 15: Social Reproduction, So Far . . .

Unlike a bicycle that can be kept in its shed for a while, capitalism is never at rest: it only exists if it expands.

Social reproduction depends on the relation between the fundamental constituents of capitalist society. There's no objective limit here. Labour may go on accepting its lot with 10 percent unemployed as with 1 percent, and the bourgeois can go on being bourgeois even if the "average" profit rate goes down to 1 percent, because global or average figures have meaning for the statistician, not for social groups. War brings fortunes to some, huge losses to others. There are times when the bourgeois will accept a 1 percent or 0 percent profit if they hope thereby to continue being a bourgeois, and times when 10 percent is not enough, and they'll risk their money and position to get an unsustainable 15 percent: then the break-even point becomes a breaking point. Capitalism is ruled by the law of profit, and its crises by "diminishing returns," but this diminishing can hardly be quantified. This is why there have been very few figures in a study that wishes to assess the break in the social balance, viz. the contradictions able to shape and shake up a whole epoch.

(a) Which irreproducibility are we talking about? Capitalism does not render its own production relationships null and void. No internal structural contradiction will be enough to do away with capitalism. To speak like Marx, its "immanent barriers" do not stop its course, they compel it to adjust: they rejuvenate it. The system's social reproduction remains possible if bourgeois and proletarians let it go on.

(b) Only communist revolution can achieve capitalism's nonreproducibility, if and when proletarians (those with jobs and those without) abolish themselves as workers.

(c) So far nothing shows that present multiple proletarian actions (defensive and offensive) point or lead to a questioning and overthrow of the capital/labour relationship.

(d) Therefore, capitalism nowadays has the means to reproduce itself. But as its long-term profitability deficit combines with growing geopolitical destabilisation aggravated by globalisation, its reproduction can only occur through disruption, violence, and more poverty. Stalemate creates an ever more explosive situation, and present austerity now imposed on countries like Greece is a mild indicator of troubled times to come.

***

"The workers' movement has not to expect a final catastrophe, but many catastrophes, political—like wars, and economic—like the crises which repeatedly break out, sometimes regularly, sometimes irregularly, but which on the whole, with the growing size of capitalism, become more and more devastating. And should the present crisis abate, new crises and new struggles will arise," Anton Pannekoek wrote in 1934, before reaching his conclusion: "The self-emancipation of the proletariat is the collapse of capitalism." Today, unless revolution does away with a system that reactivates itself by periodic self-mutilation, we are in for more extreme and devastating solutions.[15]

Anton had a point: the question is the proletariat . . . see next chapter.

CHAPTER 5

■ TROUBLE IN CLASS

As seen in the previous chapter, globalisation has been a very partial remedy to a twofold crisis: a "classical" crisis of the conditions of value production and accumulation, caused by the end of an out-of-date compromise between labour and capital; and a "civilisation" crisis, connected to the former, caused by the unbound industrialisation and mercantilisation which have given capitalism its impetus for two centuries, but which capitalism must now master to perpetuate itself. The conjunction of these aspects probably explains why the two main protagonists, the bourgeoisie and the proletariat, are reluctant to take a plunge that involves so much. Hence the freewheeling of the bourgeois, and the proletarians' divided self-defence.

§ 1: Resistance

1.1: The Autonomy Paradox
Since the early days of industrialisation, no big social gain has ever been won without spontaneous mass initiative at the grassroots level. Nearly all important reform or insurrectionary movements were launched outside institutions or by small minorities against established organisations: Chartism, English trade unionism at the end of the nineteenth century, the strike wave after World War I, the fall of the German monarchy in 1918, the anti-putsch rising in Spain in 1936, opposition to colonial wars, 1968 in France, abortion rights, and so on. While the action gathers momentum, those at the bottom manage to keep a degree of control on the running of things, until a preexisting or emerging leadership takes the matter into its separate

hands. To use fashionable words, top-down follows bottom-up. Autonomy is a sine qua non condition of efficient action for reform: in the old days of English trade unionism, shop stewards were powerless when the rank and file did not exercise its own independent pressure on the boss . . . and on them. "The emancipation of the working classes must be conquered by the working classes themselves," the First International proclaimed in 1864. We could equally say: Consistent *reform* for the working classes must be won by the working classes themselves.

"So the paradox is without the threat of revolution, reformism is a nonstarter. On the other hand, with an unruly mob on the streets and a strike-prone workforce, those reasoned reformists all of a sudden look like workable negotiation partners to whoever's in government."[1]

Autonomous action of course varies in time and space. In 1850 Manchester, self-organisation often included creating a union as an instrument that allowed labour a degree of autonomy from bourgeois power. A century later in Manchester, the rank and file had to confront both boss *and union* to lead a resolute struggle: autonomy would take the form of general meetings, an elected strike committee, control over delegates, and so on. But today, the possibilities and necessities of self-organisation differ in Wolfsburg, Germany, where the union is a lifeless bureaucratic machine, and in a Shenzhen container port, where winning union rights can be positive to worker autonomy.

It is inevitable to mistake new ways and means of labour defence against capital as the coming of a new phase when labour would attack capitalism itself. In the 1930s, it was understandable to interpret the strike and factory occupation surge in Europe and the United States, and the unskilled worker organisation that went with it, as the dawning of a new proletarian era. Subsequent events proved that industrial unions (the CIO) were far better suited to the Taylorised mass than the AFL craft unions: yet the CIO *was unionism*.[2] A new form of struggle only has revolutionary potential if the struggle starts questioning the labour-capital structure, and no form in itself (not even armed insurrection) guarantees that the action is trying to do this.

Autonomy surely is a sine qua non prerequisite of revolution: it is neither a sufficient one nor one that expresses its full content.

1.2: Autonomy/Communisation

Since 1980, worker defeat—highlighted by landmarks such as the failure of the Fiat strike in 1980, the firing of thousands of striking U.S. air traffic controllers the following year, and the division and dislocation of the British mining community in 1984–85—has been confirmed, demonstrated by work intensification, unemployment, wage freezes, reduced social entitlements and pensions, and public cuts. But unlike twenty or fifteen years ago, this worsening is met with a more systematic and more conscious resistance. One of the turning points was the 1997 UPS strike, and another was the mobilisation in 2006 of up to five million migrant workers and supporters taking to the streets in over a hundred U.S. cities (probably the largest ever worker demonstration in that country). There have been violent strikes, unlawfulness (real or staged) in the workplace, numerous wildcat strikes, huge demos against pension schemes from the Pacific to Western Europe, an insurrectional situation in Argentina for a year, riots in China to the point of setting the factory on fire and killing the manager, strikes by Bangladeshi textile workers and Spanish metal workers, direct action in sectors often deemed incapable of self-organisation (hotel personnel, farmhands in Florida, Los Angeles cleaners, as well as jobless and temp workers), riots at the periphery of Europe (Albania in 1997, Bosnia in 2014), with a return of a discourse that targets "capitalism." (A special mention for the 2006 "revolt of the penguins" in Chile, when a million young people went on strike, occupied high schools and universities, repeatedly demonstrated and clashed with the police.) In fact, there seems to be more happening every year.

What the '68 and post-'68 movement, not just in France and probably more in Italy than anywhere else, set as its objective: *self-organisation*, has now become frequent practice. While union and party machinery usually takes care of negotiations, the action properly speaking is taken on by its participants to a much bigger extent than a few decades ago. Militant strikes often have their own coordinating body outside union control, and internet sites where the strikers speak for themselves. The Iraqi *shuras* (the Arabic word for councils or consultations) took possession of villages and towns, chased the bourgeois and policemen away, and ran the place until the State army came back in force. Latin American rebels call themselves *auto-convocados* (self-organised). In 2001–2002, Argentinean proletarians self-managed hundreds of plants and set up communities based on the workshop, on neighbourhood mutual help, on swaps and bartering. As the Brazilian landless peasants say, "Occupy, Resist, Produce." The protracted insurrection of Oaxaca in Mexico, 2006, coordinated hundreds of thousands in a pyramid of grassroots collectives.

But the present movements do not go beyond self-government. In spite of its dynamism, social critique has not criticised its limits: on the contrary, it treats them as its objective. If *communisation* means the withering of commodity exchange, the upheaval of productive systems and of the whole of daily life, as well as the destruction of the State, communisation is not yet on the agenda. What was the peak and the termination of the proletarian surge in 1977: *autonomy*, is now the implicit programme of the early twenty-first-century proletarians. Conflict is intense but does not tear deep into the social fabric.

1.3: Labour Movement Resurgence

Industrialisation, and the labour concentrations it creates in huge plants and extended neighbourhoods, always causes—or revives—a worker movement. In some countries, the rise is indeed a return to former class and factory struggles, as in China, where blue-collar workers fought and were defeated in the 1920s. This is true in Latin America, Asia, and to a smaller degree Africa (South Africa and Nigeria, especially). As the proletarians in the old capitalist metropolises were defeated, those in the "emerging" countries stood up and fought, with whatever means available and various outcomes.

For instance, South Korea went through class conflicts under a semidictatorship until the late 1980s, and this has continued under democracy. The working class fights back, particularly against privatisation and anti-strike legislation. In late 2013, a police raid on the Korean Confederation of Trade Unions headquarters resulted in hundreds injured and many arrests.

In South Africa, struggles have developed before and since the end of apartheid, paralleled by the growth of unions, notably the COSATU, which engaged in a Tripartite Alliance with the CP and the (ruling party) ANC, in a classic "bourgeois government + worker bureaucracy" association. In 2012, the NUM (main miners' union) shot two of its own wildcat-striking members at Marikana, and sided with the police when they killed over thirty miners. Since then, the NUM is reported to have lost half of its membership. Wildcat strikes conflict with blatant class collaborationism, but in a country with little means of softening the blows of social strife, the antagonism rises to extremes, to a high degree of no-holds-barred violence, from the bourgeois as well as from the bureaucrats. In the United States, union bosses never refrain from "gangster" methods against their rank and file when their power and privileges are threatened. An ex-"Third World" country is following in the footsteps of "advanced" democracies.

Latin America offers contrasting examples of worker movement maturation. In Brazil, the Workers' Party (PT) launched in 1980, became the largest party in parliament, got ex-metalworker Lula twice elected president (2002–2011), and when in power has done its best to integrate Brazil into globalisation while alleviating its impact upon the poor. Chávez's Bolivarian socialism, on the other hand, played the radical score of wealth redistribution and anti-imperialist confrontation. Two seemingly diametrically opposed politics, yet both compatible with world capitalism and national class equilibrium, Brazil in a moderate centre-left way that pleases European and U.S. liberals, Venezuela with a far-left posturing that appeals to radicals.

The emergence of India on the world market has given a fresh momentum to a century-old tradition of labour struggle and organisation. If one of the main demands is the right to unionise, it is because unions are perceived as a useful instrument to press for demands. A special but not exceptional example was a four-month strike in 2011, in the Maruti Suzuki car factory (near Delhi, with 70 percent casual labour: a usual proportion in the Indian automotive industry). Strikers' demands were primarily union recognition, plus other grievances: they were locked out, fought back by occupying the premises twice, until they reached a compromise with the bosses.[3]

In this situation and similar ones (Bangladeshi textile workers, for example, who are paid scant wages), a combative rank-and-file strikes and riots, often achieves Pyrrhic victories, and creates or rejuvenates official labour institutions that specialise in capital-labour bargaining and function as shock absorbers to cushion the struggles. The bourgeois are forced to accept a (re)nascent trade-union movement while they limit the right to strike by forbidding solidarity pickets, sympathetic strikes, striking with "political" aims, and so on, not forgetting riot police and death squads. Nevertheless, you can do anything with a bayonet except sit on it. Workers are always able to put some spanner or other in the works, so repression cannot be the only way of dealing with labour.

1.4: Proletarian Drive and Bourgeois Outcome

Masses draw their energy from their material conditions.

Then, usually, after a while, this indisputable proletarian content moves to the background.

In Spain, July 1936, if workers were more numerous than teachers in the armed resistance to the military coup, it was because the working class was used to defending (sometimes with guns) its own interests against the State and the bourgeois. They did not take to the streets in support of a parliamentary regime. Since 2011, Arab masses have not been fighting *for* democracy. That was neither the cause of their mobilising nor of their standing fast. Millions were spurred into demonstrations and riots because their plight (economic exploitation and political oppression) had got worse: price increase of staples like flour, rice, gas, and lower wages. This chain of circumstances can be verified throughout history, in the periods preceding 1789 or 1848. When a regime has exhausted its capacities, even for misrule, then a minor factor—a corruption scandal, a military setback, an over-the-top police repression, or a socially significant suicide like in Tunisia—is enough to trigger mass reaction.

Those who risk their own lives are fighting as "no reserves," propertyless people. They are not supporting the liberal reform-minded bourgeoisie: their interests are in opposition to those of property and money. For them, free speech and access to education, health and welfare are part of a fundamental demand: the possibility to live, which is denied to them because they are deprived of inherited means of livelihood, and forced to earn a living by selling their labour. Politically, a consistent defence of their interests leads them into direct conflict with the State, not into parliamentary options. For them, being able to meet publicly, to speak out, to organise, to read the paper they choose, to write and distribute a leaflet, to stop work, to march in the street, is a condition of a social struggle that antagonises the dominant sectors of the anti-dictatorship camp. The bourgeois rarely mind a dictator as long as they can go on with their business, and for them democratic rights hardly mean possibilities of free labour organisation. On the contrary, it is *that* freedom which the proletarians win, albeit briefly, when demos and riots topple a reactionary regime. There resides the deep cause that motivates them and fuels social and political energy.

How the insurgents use that freedom is a different matter. The fact that proletarian interests activated the events does not automatically turn these interests into *objectives* that the proletarians would do their best to implement. For instance, as in post-1789 France, they might press for price regulation, requisition, taxes on the rich, subsidies on staples, even some dose of what is now called planning. No such programme was put forward by the rioters at the time of the Arab Spring, let alone since. As society and power abhor a vacuum, the political void can be filled with a variety of contents, religion being one of them. Islamists often win elections in areas where they become popular by compensating for the public deficiencies regarding health, schooling, and welfare. This explains why Suez Islamists did quite well in the general election that followed the ousting of Mubarak, though everybody knew they had played very little part in the local riots.

Proletarian uprisings on other continents, notably in Asia, would provide us with other examples of the contradiction between the initial energy and the course of its development.[4] Collective creativity, risk-taking, inventiveness, fraternity, the freeing of speech, contribute to a vibrant community of struggle ... which does not reach the threshold where it would not just clash with the State and the capital-labour relation but would start overturning them. Though proletarians are ready to die confronting powers that tower above them, they do not set up neighbourhood and workplace counterpower organs that would organise an altogether different life. They still put their trust in others than themselves. Social movements are immensely rich, but not yet rich of transformative communist will.

§ 2: Going Beyond Class?

2.1 Occupy/Transform

The nearly worldwide "Occupy," "Squares," and *indignants* movements have been interpreted as endeavours to overpass *class*, in the sense that they do not lock themselves up in work issues and in (soft or hard) capital-labour bargaining. In fact, up to now, these movements have usually reacted against anti-labour and anti-social *government* measures, and have rarely related to conflicts simultaneously happening in workplaces. By and large, they have brought people together.

This points more to a crisis *within* class relations than to a crisis *of* class relations—a crisis that might initiate the destruction of class structure. Present unrest acts as if it could absorb class without doing away with what maintains it: the capital-labour opposition. Togetherness is a necessary dimension of revolution, *providing* it breaks with class division, not when it fuses class groups into an aggregate mass. On Tahrir, Puerta del Sol, Taksim . . . the fact that those without any means of livelihood have to sell their labour power to those who organise work and profit from it, in simpler words the basic fact of exploitation, was interpreted in terms of poor v. rich, powerless v. powerful, bottom v. top. Therefore the solution could only be a fair resharing of wealth and power.

We are not suggesting everything will be fine the day the Cairote jobless refuse to demonstrate alongside doctors because proletarians don't associate with middle class. The question is what they *do* and *cannot do* together. The shift from factory to street occupation, from private to public places, is immensely positive if occupiers transform what they take over: one has to get hold of something before transforming it. But takeover is not ipso facto changeover. The reclaiming of public space signifies a will to reappropriate our lives, an intuition that production and work should not be central in our lives: that could be a starting point for a critique of the economy and work, if production and work were confronted and not bypassed. Otherwise, just as the occupied factory occupies its occupiers and keeps them within the confines of labour issues, those who occupy the square immerse themselves in the occupation tasks. Solidarity is an indispensable dimension of revolutionary breakthrough, a part, not the whole, and when the part replaces the whole, community becomes an end in itself. A Madrid participant was saying in May 2012: "People are fighting to take decisions themselves." What *self* is meant and, what's more, *which* decisions?

True, the more entrenched and enclosed in bargaining labour stays, the more it is stuck in the workplace, physically or mentally: factory or office walls are more than bricks, they also permeate minds and attitudes. But being far away from factory gates is not enough for a rejection of work. In the Occupy movement, as the critique remained on the surface of things, its lack of in-depth content enabled vital necessities such as sharing and autonomy to be reduced to ideologies: mass horizontal action became a programme in its own right.

Workerism was an impasse, and we won't feel regret for a time when activists were ashamed of their uncalloused hands.

This is no reason for swapping one dead-end with another. Masses of proletarianised ex-middle class people will not automatically coalesce into the revolutionary subject that factory work is now deemed unable to create. All-togetherness has no intrinsic subversive virtue. Even when it evades bureaucratic control, acting together is not self-sufficient: it only undermines law and order when it opens up onto something qualitatively different.

Community life and action in the same space develop a self-governing urban locus and its creative energy. Like riots, occupations have a generative power, and they are privileged moments of the birth of the *social individual*: participants cease to be alone without dissolving their personality. (They are not spectators as when attending a political meeting or a football match.) This process is a condition of a quantum leap: a necessary condition, not a sufficient one. Popular resistance is a threat to capitalism: it will not pull it apart.

Sharing food, clothes, first aid, child care, and money builds and consolidates an interacting collective, with a caveat: money-sharing breaks with value-count, as the richer occupier will give to the poorer, but generosity does not do away with money, nor is it meant to: the implicit (or sometimes explicit) perspective is not a moneyless world, simply equalisation.[5]

In radical circles, critics of the Occupy movement have insisted on its middle class composition. This seems sociologically undeniable, but the litmus test is not so much the small proportion of workers in the events, rather the rarity of interchange and synergy between public space occupation and labour struggles going on at the time. The poverty of cross-pollination between different (and divided) proletarian categories was also true of the 2005 French *banlieue* riots. In the 2008 Greek rising, there was some—but little—connection between casual labour or jobless participants, and factory or more stable labour.

Using public space as a social weapon is an old and widespread phenomenon. The Indian *bandh* (meaning "closed") is a combination of an often local general strike, blockade, and neighbourhood takeover to protest against an injustice or to support a demand. Nobody goes to work, shops do not open, public transport stops, and a whole district—sometimes a city— will be off-limits for a few hours or days. The locals block the roads to keep authority representatives outside, and create their own temporary time-space to put forward minor or major grievances, in a cocktail of civil disobedience and violence (stoning, arson, burglary). Class lines are blurred as shopkeepers fight alongside their employees. How much of this is community self-defence? How much could this community self-transform? One does not necessarily lead to the other. A cross-class aggregate does not supersede class. Resisting oppression and exploitation is a first step to getting rid of them . . . only the first.

2.2: Radical-Reformist Complication

At the time of writing, the Greek rebellion in 2008 remains the peak of the social movement in Europe since the 1970s. Yet even there, "contradictory dynamics" prevailed, "its majority tendency was a reformist one," and "renewed, among other things, the social-democratic demand for "stable and permanent work." Therefore: "In this struggle, as in many other cases in the history of capitalism, the radical and the reformist tendency coexisted at the same time."[6]

In spite (and because) of the overall trend toward impoverishment, demands are being put forward, sometimes with partial success. Asian strikes and riots have resulted in 10 to 20 percent wage rises. In the early 1920s, it was not uncommon for Chinese labour to get as much as 50 percent: whether these increases were to last was another matter, but they were not economically absurd: when workers are paid literally starvation wages, reproduction of the labour force is impossible.

Nowadays, in the old industrial heartland, Germany for instance, as they are unable to agitate for better wages or work conditions, laid-off workers press for as much severance pay as they can snatch (up to $100,000 in some cases). Far from being a sign of a critique of one's proletarian condition, it is the only possible proletarian demand left.

Chapter 1 recalled how the 1960s–70s proletarian offensive in the "old" capitalist metropolises did not develop anything resembling the traditional worker movement, even in new forms (as new today as the CPs new-style reformism or the CIO reinvented unionism were new in the 1930s). Since then, however, as summed up above in § 1.3, a labour movement has grown in other areas.

As long as capitalism exists, and in the direst of circumstances, labour will confront capital, find means of applying pressure to match that of the boss, and never put an end to defensive (i.e., reformist) endeavours, by traditional or innovative means. Proletarians do not pursue "all-or-nothing" policies.

The contradiction between reformist organisations and radical minorities, which is also a conflict within the proletarians, and even within each proletarian between moderation and radicalism, will go on persisting up to even more stormy times.

§ 3: Communism as Ideology

Understandably, *communism* has got itself a bad name, and it is likely that most of those who now label themselves "communists" are either nostalgic revivalists of East Germany or of the Shining Path in Peru (there's a virtual galaxy of them on the Web), or gravely confused, in any case people light years away from the points made in this book.

Yet it is obviously possible to speak about communism without using the word, or even while rejecting the word. So let's consider not the vocabulary but what radicalism targets today.

Compared to what it used to be, social critique now appears closer to communism. No one expects a rosy future from (even soviet-managed) mass electrification: in fact, those who speak about soviets would rather have them *without* big power stations. It's common to question industrial development, to wish for conditions of existence that aren't given to us from above by a State or an omnipotent technical complex, but by a multitude of self-reliant horizontally connected communities. This is positive, but . . .

Though a DIY collective practice is a condition of communist revolution, it says little about its substance.

Contemporary *zeitgeist* reflects the evolution of a capitalism that cannot evade the issue of its own cancerous growth, in the same way as the dream of a megamachine able to fulfil all our needs reflected the technological optimism of 1950. One common wisdom (or one illusion) has been replaced by another. Politicians praise *low-carbon* development, the oil peak makes the news, and "quality" and "popular" papers alike prefer soft to hard technology. There's little merit in rejecting overgrowth when lucid bourgeois write about the excesses of capital accumulation. Most critical theory does not counteract prevailing ideas: it runs parallel to them. If the "spectre of communism" haunts the world, it is in ideological form: communal life, mutual help, grassroots self-organisation . . . all those elements partake of communisation, except they are ideologised when disconnected from the basic realities which command the whole system (and its possible change).[7] Communism may exist as a widespread desire for a Stateless, moneyless and wageless world, but it now rarely goes beyond the level of desire—hardly more than in former times, anyway.

§ 4: The Improbable Art of Crisis Assessment

Why were the 1920 events better understood in 1950 than in 1920? Because in 1950 people knew the consequences of 1920 that those who lived through the 1920s of course could not foresee. The change is more than factual: it entails a new point of view. Each generation rewrites the history of the previous period.

To understand turning and tipping points, one has to grasp small-scale yet significant aspects that are portents of change . . . with the risk of inflating their importance and mistaking the part for the whole. The difficulty is to highlight the facts that are auspicious *for the future* without neglecting those that are *still now* prevailing, otherwise we turn the exception into the rule.

It would be too simple if all fighting categories converged automatically just because they have one common cause: world capital. Sharing the same cause does not necessarily entail targeting it together. Our problem is not the existence or development of struggles: they are more numerous and remarkable than all indymedia sites combined will ever tell us, and their blossoming does not depend on theorists or activists. There are and there will be insurrections. But communist ones? . . . As we know, crisis and tension *also* beget antihuman and anticommunist conflicts and responses. Law and order is counterrevolutionary: disorder can be too. Very few civil wars now taking place on this planet qualify as progressive steps to emancipation. With the deepening and worsening of the current situation, hundreds of millions of proletarians may find themselves with nothing to lose, yet *not* initiate a communist effort.

> A class must be formed which has radical chains, a class in civil society which is not a class of civil society, a class which is the dissolution of all classes, a sphere of society which has universal character because its sufferings are universal, and which does not claim a particular redress because the wrong which is done to it is not a particular wrong but wrong in general. There must be formed a sphere of society which claims no traditional status but only a human status. . . . This dissolution of society, as a particular class, is the proletariat. (*A Contribution to a Critique of Hegel's Philosophy of Right*, Introduction, 1844)

Fine reading, which still has to be realised. Until then, we'll have workers asking for more wages and better work conditions, or fighting a factory closure. We'll have occupiers aiming at festive solidarity and community. We'll have riots like in Greece, 2008. We'll have South American laid-off workers block a bridge to get better severance pay. Or Indian villagers *bandhing* to block the area against a rise in the price of petrol. So far all these forms of resistance fight separately, or at best side by side, they react to "the encroachments of capital" but do not converge in such a way as to transform what they do and transform *themselves.*

§ 5: No Revolutionary Subject without Subjectivity

Crisis times have a double characteristic. Circumstances become more compellingly objective, because they reduce the scope of "usual" possibilities: there are less jobs, less money, less opportunities. At the same time, a variety of "unusual" options open up, ranging from despair, outright reaction, religious withdrawal to rebellion. Turmoil calls for a different degree of freedom from normality. Taking part in or staying away from strike, demonstration, local initiative, roadblock, occupation, riot, and barricade, meeting new people and challenging one's identity, past and ideas, all these imply personal and collective choices.

Our previous chapter ended with what Pannekoek wrote in 1934: "The self-emancipation of the proletariat is the breakdown of capitalism." It is significant the quote should come as the conclusion of *The Theory of the Breakdown of Capitalism,* which studies how this system "naturally" breeds crises. So the same text that ponders over the inner contradictions of capitalism declares that only proletarian activity will get rid of that system. This duality requires some explanation.

From the 1840s onward, unlike utopian socialists that appealed to morals, to bourgeois good will or to worker idealism, communism has wished to found itself on the historical grounds created by capitalism, because this system gives "modern" proletarians the ability to make a revolution that formerly the exploited could not and would not make.

> And if these material elements of a complete revolution are not present (namely, on the one hand the existing productive forces, on the other the formation of a revolutionary mass, which revolts not only against separate conditions of society up till then, but against the very "production of life" till then, the "total activity" on which it was based), then, as

far as practical development is concerned, it is absolutely immaterial whether the idea of this revolution has been expressed a hundred times already, as the history of communism proves. (*The German Ideology*, Part I. B)

On the eve of 1914, when Rosa Luxemburg set out to prove the inevitability of a final crisis in *The Accumulation of Capital* (1913), she did not expect revolution to derive from this crisis, as an effect unavoidably follows its cause. She thought capitalism was inevitably heading toward destruction and war, but not inevitably to its self-destruction: its overthrow would result from the conscious action of the exploited.[8] Twenty years later, as Pannekoek was writing in the midst of a world crisis on a scale hitherto unknown but which coincided with the triumph of Hitler and Stalin, he made it clear that capitalism brings about the possibility of human emancipation, not its certainty.

History is made by conscious acts, which involve decisions . . . which are not based on free will. It would be pointless to replace nineteenth-century determinism (based on a widespread belief in progress, shared by bourgeois and socialists alike) by contemporary undeterminism (influenced by the cultural pessimism of a self-doubting society).

Revolution is neither the fruit of long-cultivated undermining action, nor of will power. It was off the agenda in 1852, in 1872, or in 1945 (although some comrades mistook the end of World War II for the dawning of a new Red October). Not everything is possible at any given time. Critical moments give opportunities: it depends on the proletarians, it depends on us to exploit these capabilities. Nothing guarantees the coming of a communist revolution, nor its success if it comes. A historical movement keeps developing because its participants make it do so. A revolution withers when people stop believing in it and no longer rise to the challenge they have initiated. History is not to be understood with the mind of the chemist analysing molecular reactions. The closer communist theory gets to "science," the less communist it becomes. Communism is not to be proved.

CHAPTER 6

■ CREATIVE INSURRECTION

We are not talking about a plan to be fulfilled one day, a project adequate to the needs of the proletarians (and ultimately of humankind) but exterior to them, like blueprints on the architect's drawing board before the house is built. Communisation depends on what the proletarian *is* and *does*.

§ 1: An Anti-work and Anti-proletarian Insurrection?

1.1: Self-Critique of Work

If work has such a hold on us, it is not the result of bourgeois brainwashing. Workers are practical: they know work brings in money, sometimes comes with comradeship and solidarity, and gives a semblance of meaning to life. Even boring jobs may have a minimum social sense. A tollbooth collector was telling how she gets to know drivers who pass her booth twice a day and occasionally have a little chat with her and bring her presents. This paltry relationship does not nullify the drudgery of work or the fact that few workers actually *enjoy* their job. For most, especially when unemployment is high, what matters is getting *a job* to "earn a living." There is no acquired work love among proletarians that would be a major obstacle on the way to revolution. Any turbulent period reveals to its participants that their need of having a purpose and a community could be fulfilled differently. Insurrection brings a personal and collective break with ingrained habits.

Until then, it is inevitable for the demand for work and for job-creation to be fairly common, and for many to react like the Belgian Arcelor Mittal laid-off employee who was saying in 2012: "With metal, Lakshmi Mittal does not make sheet steel, he makes money. What a waste!" Ideally for this employee steelmaking should be, primarily, job-creating. Up to now, most redundant workers protest against unemployment, not against work. Revolution would be a rejection of both.

In the 1960s, strikers would often fight for "time to live": fewer working hours and more free time. This indeed *qualitative* claim accepted capitalist domination and attempted to reduce its scope. We now sometimes hear a differently qualitative slogan: "It's not a living we want, it's a life."

Communist insurrection would happen at the junction where struggles led by overexploited people (starvation wages—sometimes unpaid, lack of safety measures, denial of labour laws, fines at the boss's whim, management dictatorship and systematic repression), meet struggles involving proletarians employed under "softer" conditions in "protected" jobs. Though the first category is widespread in Asia, Latin America, or Africa, both categories coexist in North America, Europe, and Japan, so the junction will not occur between continents but within countries. The critique of wage-labour and work will be born out of the joint refusal of outright misery caused by jobless-ness and wage or pension cuts, and of the illusory safety and consumption that capitalism sells or promises.

Communist insurrection will fuse struggles against exploitation *and* alienation, critiques of poverty *and* of wealth: the insurgents at the same time will ask for what they don't have *and* refuse what they are being offered. There's obviously a contradiction here, between demanding and rejecting, but historical examples show this contradiction can be superseded. Italian workers in the 1970s used to disrupt or sabotage produc- tion to the point of jeopardising the running of the factory and threatening their own livelihood. They reached a stage when fighting for demands was beginning to lose its relevance com- pared to a possible questioning of the labour/capital couple. The offensive stood at a crossroads. It could either move up from the negative to the positive, from destructive local insubordination to active global refusal, by going outside the factory into the neighbourhood, initiating nonmercantile relationships, destroying work as a separate sphere and confronting the State, which meant expanding its scope and transforming riots into insurrection. Or the workforce could use factory unrest to get the most out of the management in the ensuing collective bargaining. This is the way the struggle went in the 1970s. The question of the self-suppression of the proletarian condition (and of capitalism) was posed and left unanswered: the movement withered until the contradiction was finally resolved by capital's reengineering.

Anti-work happens at a moment when labour does not fight *as labour* anymore: workers no longer "respect" machines, they disregard the production schedule and the perpetuation of the company, which means putting their jobs at risk. It is never just a "human" rebellion, it has historical causes: in the 1970s, mass unskilled workers reacted to the extremes of Fordism and the intensification of the work process. "Anti-work" was different in 1860 and 1960, and differs again in the early twenty-first century. It is not something that radicals should promote as the new lever strong enough to move the world. But one sign of the coming of a revolutionary period will be an increased number of anti-work acts, first launched by small minorities, then becoming more and more common.

1.2: Anti-proletarian Acts

What has been called *anti-proletarian* does not take on just the workplace, also where the proletarians live.[1] For instance, rioters destroy buildings which are instruments and symbols of the domination imposed upon them: police stations, tax offices, supermarkets, banks, estate, and temp agencies, but also public places such as schools, libraries, cultural centres, and public means of transport (geared to work).

As the media hasten to say, devastating or burning down these places and vehicles goes against the immediate interest of the local population. If the riot sets about them, however, there is more to it than sheer nihilist frenzy: these places stand for and are indeed means of reproducing a social system the rioters reject, school for a start. And what proportion of the lower classes frequent the art centre and the public library? There is ambiguity here, obviously. In the French Revolution, women enraged by the dearness and rarity of foodstuffs would sometimes smash eggs on market stalls. It is irrational for hungry people to waste food: these women's rationality was neither alimentary nor economic. A few years ago, in a South African shanty town, rioters set fire to some of their few available public services: a library and wooden poles about to be used to extend the electric network. In Bangladesh, woman workers assisted by the locals torched a factory that was their only way to "earn a living."

The self-abolition of the proletariat implies the destruction of conditions of life that both *control* and *protect* the proletarians, blocks of flats and public amenities for instance. Both functions are intricately interwoven and it is impossible to completely distinguish the "bad" from the "good," control from protection.

No social movement is crystal pure, even less so in violent times. Mercedes showrooms will go up in flames, possibly also a store of bed linen. The extension of communisation and proletarians' control of their own violence are the sole guarantee that such waste will remain an isolated event, and that excess and purely negative rampage will be avoided, limited, or prevented. An expanding geography of freedom comes with intraproletarian conflict. When "you're burning your houses, burning the streets, with anxiety," as the Ruts sang in 1979, the arsonist might clash with the inflamed. There is no revolution without disorder: our problem will be to see to it that a new socialisation comes out of de-socialisation. Otherwise riots only reproduce themselves, proletarian self-destruction remains negative, police-free zones become the hunting ground of gangs, the impetus tires out, inertia sets in, and sooner or later the old order is back.

§ 2: From Work to Activity?

Communist revolution is the superseding of "quantitative" and "qualitative" struggles, the end of the opposition between bread-and-butter issues and a revolt against daily life. That process will not be initiated unless a large part of production comes to a halt.

To understand what insurgents can do, we must start from what they are: "no reserve" people. Not all proletarians are exploited as workers, some are only occasionally or casually employed, some are rarely given a job, but all are submitted to capital because labour is what has been deprived of means of livelihood and is forced to sell itself for a wage. In the best of cases, the *affluent worker* only owns the house he lives in and has little money in the bank.[2] In that sense, the growth of worldwide middle-classness is a myth. In fact, throughout history, when civil war is looming or their position is threatened, the real moneyed classes have been known to leave the city and send their family to the country or abroad: even if he wanted to, the bus driver, cleaner or schoolteacher can't. This is class difference.

Because they are separated from resources to live on, and *collectively* so, the insurgent proletarians cannot rely on savings, capital, public support or rich foreign friends. They can either go back to the fold of submission after a festive break (anthropologists liken this to the carnival tradition of putting the world upside down for a day), or they can start implementing something radically different. The solution to collective dispossession is to get a hold on what exists (goods, the productive system), but which the insurgents cannot use as bourgeois would—they have no "funds," no capital, no business connections, no State backing—so the only way to succeed, and simply to resist anti-insurrection forces, is to invent something different from work, money and the economy.

In an industrial combine like the one of Foxconn in China, where over 150,000 migrant workers manufacture electronic goods, insurgent workers could have no hope of keeping on making the same items and having them shipped all over the world: assuming they tried, international business would not allow it. The Foxconn industrial site is a monster the proletarians could do nothing with, except seize the place, first to find ways of surviving and fighting. Most workers would leave. Those who would stay would close or pull down most of the factories and dormitories, only keep the equipment necessary to produce what can improve the quality of life, and begin a new relation between town and country, industry and agriculture. This would not be a new mode of production, because production—by which we do not mean techniques but production relations—would not rule life.

Mass worker stoppages are indispensable to revolution, and they include strikes and blockades.

Blockades target focal points: shopping centres, commuter hubs, fuel depots . . . In a *just in time* and *zero stock* society, cutting off lines of communication is as efficient as stopping assembly lines. The end of huge factories in Europe (not in Asia) has coincided with more (and not less) industrial concentration. In the north of France, with a work force of 3,250, the Française de Mécanique makes 5 percent of all light vehicle engines manufactured in the world. The plant was blocked for a couple of hours in 2010, as part of a nationwide protest against pension cuts. The protest was eventually ineffectual, and the union-controlled blockade more symbolic than antagonistic, but it shows the potential power given to two hundred people by the modern economy.

Strikes and blockades go together: it would be an illusion to replace the former by the latter, on the grounds that because productive work is deemed unessential, workplace action should now give way to blocking circulation and distribution. This notion is an internalisation of how contemporary capitalism pictures itself: a world of flows. Yet we live in a *stock and flow* society. This also internalises the *present* condition of labour in the United States and Europe, where unemployment and downsizing make strike action difficult. Moreover, replacing workplace by public space is no solution. If money and boss pressures are strong enough to deter people from acting where they work, how will they be able to leave their shop floor or office and go out to block a fuel depot? Action both inside and outside the workplace is necessary to have an effect on society.

There has been a difference so far between *piqueteros* and European blockers. In Latin America, a piquet is often the cause and effect of a collective that gets organised, debates, goes beyond the framework of its action, and initiates dynamics that could lead further. It has something of a soviet, a council, an action committee, an assembly in the Spanish 1970s sense: this autonomy is a condition that enables more than itself, more than its initial goal. In future times, a synthesis of strike and blockade will be a way of going beyond class: their respective participants—a compound of people with jobs and without, schoolchildren, housewives, students—will cease to be sociologically defined by what they used to be. Their acting together will start creating new productive and living relations, and inaugurate a move from *work* to *activity*.

To avoid playing with words, let us be clear on what work is.

Work is not producing objects. When someone with DIY abilities and the necessary tools makes a table for their home, the table corresponds to their means and needs. On the contrary, the professional carpenter makes a certain range of tables and could not afford to take into account all specific needs. Neither can a furniture factory. To meet demand, the private producer designs an item that must be used as a table in a variety of situations which he only knows via market studies. This has nothing to do with the fact that hundreds of different sizes, shapes, and colours of tables are available in big stores or online. The age is gone when Henry Ford said that customers could have their car painted any color they wanted so long as it was black. Myriads of standards do not diminish the rule of cost-cutting standardisation, they just complicate it: no table is made as *a* table, all are made as exchangeable commodities. To be sold, a table must come as close as possible to a norm, and norms imply productivity and time-saving. Only artists or expensive cabinet-makers create single tables.

Normalisation is always presented as a technical necessity to mass-produce in everybody's best interest. In fact, the exchangeability of components and parts (illustrated by the French factory producing one light vehicle engine out of twenty) derives from a system based on the exchangeability of commodities, which have to be reduced to a common element, and this measurable imperative applies first and foremost to labour. Exchange (i.e., competition) determines the required productivity norm imposed upon labour.

To break with a society of social averages and figures, the insurgents will use not so much what they have as what they *are*. To make their insurrection a success—which will be a priority—they need to care about food, lodging for the homeless, transport, water, and energy supply, and be ready to fight for it all. As insurgents will be doing things for themselves and for others, abiding by the constraints of productivity, standardisation and time-count would be irrelevant. Unlike workers, they are not subordinated to the result of what they are doing. Calling him or her a *producer* would be restrictive.

We are not suggesting that communism is a DIY world where every self-sufficient (small, by necessity) community makes its own furniture and eats what vegetables it grows. We are merely outlining a revolutionary process that cannot be achieved locally but must begin locally, without waiting for regional coordination and planning to take the first steps.

Of course, there is no guarantee that future insurgents will behave this way. Italian metalworkers seized factories in 1920 and just waited. And we know what became of the only worker revolution that toppled bourgeois power in 1917. All theory can do is show what possibilities are opened up by insurrection.

§ 3: How Will Communisation Satisfy People's Basic Needs?

Nobody denies material necessities:

"In general, people cannot be liberated as long as they are unable to obtain food and drink, housing and clothing in adequate quality and quantity." (*The German Ideology*, Part I, B)

"The worst that can happen to revolutionaries is having to worry about what workers are going to eat." (letter from Marx to Engels, August 19, 1852)

As explained in chapter 3, § 2.2, what we dispute is that human life consists primarily in fulfilling needs, and that, logically, revolution should primarily consist in creating a society where physical needs are fulfilled.

Communism obviously takes basic needs into account, especially in a world where about one billion people are underfed. But how will this vital food issue be addressed? The natural urge to grow food, potatoes for instance, will be met through the birth of social links which will also result in vegetable gardening. This is no idealism: "When communist *artisans* associate with one another, theory, propaganda, etc., is their first end. But at the same time, as a result of this association, they acquire a new need—the need for society—and what appears as a means becomes an end." (*1844 Manuscripts*)

Even more so in an insurrectionary period.

Communisation will satisfy vital needs, which capitalism often does not. (Still, let's beware of calorie counts based on what is required for a hard day's work.) But that will not be its prime mover nor the cause of its coming. The necessity insurrection will respond to is not a natural (to feed oneself) one but a social one: "a new need—the need for society."

In communism, unlike in the economy, no productive act is determinant in itself. Everything has its singularity and can become debatable: building a table or a house, organising a training course or a journey. Restaurants as we know them appeared in the early nineteenth century.[3] If restaurants are abolished, how do travellers feed themselves? Phasing out work to develop human activity includes dealing with such matters, with a strong degree of local and individual initiative. How they would converge is impossible to foretell. Human activity, or *generic activity* to use Marx's term in his early writings, does not mean permanent harmony. Communism is not universal peace and love. Concord is not a given: it results from certain practices, and is negated by others, war obviously, also competition between companies, and work.

In the early days, proletarians will help each other and help themselves. The homeless will occupy empty housing and places that only have a capitalist function: banks, estate agents, business and tax office . . . Of course, here and there and for a while, shortages will be inevitable. If everything was available in warehouses, the answer would seem easy—shopping made free—but supermarkets only store a limited amount of food and basic items, especially with a *zero stock* policy. Obviously counterrevolution will make the most of undersupply and scarcity. Insurgents will have to turn shortages to their own advantage, and take the opportunity of reversing the situation by engaging in different ways of producing and circulating goods.

Sceptics have always doubted the common people's ability to satisfy their own needs without the medium of money and the leadership of wise men. A frequent answer among anarchists and communists is to insist on the artificiality of needs: the day humans live a fraternal and simpler life, they will do without a lot of what is now indispensable. In 1887, William Morris was saying that a world with no slaves would eliminate objects that are only needed by slaves. He meant junk, but his statement holds true for a number of contemporary social and cognitive electronic prostheses: one does not have to be technophobic to realise that the prime function of a lot of them is to connect people who are separated, and to do so in seconds. What used to be a business norm—always saving time—has turned into everyone's permanent mania. We can assume that the end of time-count and cost-cutting in productive activities, together with an extension of immediate direct exchange, will change our communicating habits, and decrease the urge to be constantly and immediately informed of everything.

However stimulating it is, that answer ventures on the slippery ground of the nature/artifice distinction. Humans are natural *and* artificial creatures, and it is always risky to draw a line between authenticity and manipulation, between desire and need. Besides, no-one escapes the manipulative powers of advertising, which affect the educated as much as the underclass, and it is futile to be judgemental about Londoners looting electronic gadgets in 2011, as if only looting bags of flour in Cairo was acceptable on a proletarian scale of values.

Not only are needs historically determined, but need itself is a history-bound category.

"The proletarian is the person who is separated from everything, and who enters in relation with this everything through *needs*." (*La Banquise* 2, 1983)

Although need looks like the most natural obvious fact, it belongs to the set of economic concepts. Need *is* separation.

It is the economy that *disconnects production from consumption* as two distinct realities.

Communisation changes the relation between what we know as two separate spheres:

> The "producer" doesn't leave his needs in the cloakroom. He includes in his "productive" activity his choices, his personality and the satisfaction of his needs. And vice versa, the "consumer" is not sent back to a life deprived of sociality to assume the functions of his immediate reproduction. . . .
>
> In the communist revolution, the productive act will never be *only* productive. One sign of this among others will be the fact that the product considered will be particular: it will correspond to needs expressed *personally* (by the direct producers at the time or by others) and that the satisfaction of the need won't be separated from the productive act itself. Let's think, for example, about how the construction of housing will change as soon as standardisation disappears. Production without productivity will mean that any individual engaged in the project will be in a position to give his opinion concerning the product and the methods. Things will go much slower than in today's industrialised building industry. The participants in the project may even wish to live there after the building is finished. Will it be a total mess? Let's just say that time will not count and that cases in which the project isn't completed, in which everything is abandoned in midstream—maybe because production of the inputs is without productivity too—won't be a problem. Again, this is because the activity will have found its justification in itself, independently of its productive result."[4]

To understand that *the first need of man is man* without falling into an idealist or humanistic trap, one can think of factual examples. Some Argentine *piqueteros* in 1999–2001 pioneered productions where the product was not the sole objective. This is easier to grasp with nonmaterial activities: a school does not manufacture objects (though modern productivity-geared schooling tends to churn out degrees and diplomas), it transforms the learners as well as the teachers, and creates new relationships, or should do so. But the same logic could apply to object-making. A *piquetero's* communal bakery would bake bread, *and* the productive act would be a moment of change in interindividual relationships: no leaders, consensus decision-making etc.

§ 4: Abundance v. Scarcity?

For most Marxists and quite a few anarchists, the original cause of the exploitation of man by man was the emergence of a *surplus* of production in societies still plagued by *scarcity*. The argument could be summed up as follows. For thousands of years, a minority was able to make the majority work for the benefit of a privileged few who kept most of the surplus for themselves. Fortunately, despite its horrors, capitalism is bringing about an unheard-of and ever-growing wealth: the poverty of the masses is no longer the condition for education, leisure and art to be enjoyed only by the elite.

The logical conclusion is that the goal (shared by most tendencies of the worker movement) should be a society of abundance. Against capitalism which forces us to work without fulfilling our needs, and distributes its products in most unequal fashion, revolution should organise the mass production of goods beneficial to all. And it *can*, thanks to the celebrated "development of the productive forces." In sum, revolution unbinds Prometheus.

Moreover, and this is no minor point, such a vision believes that abundance will transform humankind. When men and women are properly fed, housed, schooled, educated, cared for, "struggle for life" antagonisms and attitudes will gradually disappear, individualism will give way to altruism, and nobody will have any motive, therefore feel any desire, for greed, domination, or violence. So the only real question that remains is how to adequately manage this society of abundance. In a democratic way or via leaders? With Kropotkin's moneyless system of helping oneself to goods that are plentiful, and democratic rationed sharing-out for those goods that can't be plentiful? Or with some labour-time accounting as elaborated by the councilists in the 1930s? Whatever, the answer given by anarchists and non-Leninist communists is a society of "associated producers" run by worker collectives. All these schemes describe a different *economy*, but an economy all the same: they start from the assumption that social life is based on the necessity to allocate resources in the best possible way to produce goods.

This is precisely where we beg to differ.

A typical feature of what we have been used to calling "the economy" is to produce goods separately from needs (which may be "natural" or "artificial," authentic or manipulated, that matters but is not essential at this point), before offering them on a market where they will be bought to be consumed.

Communism is not a new "economy," even a regulated, bottom-up, decentralised, and self-managed one. We can hardly call it a new "mode of production": as seen in the previous section, production itself would change its relation to the rest of life.

Realists argue that the critique of abundance is a luxury for the rich, and that producing a lot more by modern techniques is an urgent must for the poorest countries and areas, *favelas*, slums, and shantytowns. Realists miss the point. Dire misery will not be met by bridging the gap between a "low" development level and the one already reached by "rich" countries, as if communist "development aid" came to raise "backward" zones up to advanced standards, minus of course the excesses of overgrowth (we'll build bike-tracks instead of motorways). Communisation would obviously imply solidarity, but the major impetus would come from the inhabitants of those areas themselves. Deprivation does not mean total destitution, absolute exclusion and a war of all against all: these people have proved an ability to organise and fight. Slum life is not just rooting through garbage for survival: it also invents ways of house-building and urban food-producing.

Attempts at self-help are now circumscribed and biased by their capitalist environment, but they illustrate the imaginative resources available even in unfavourable conditions. Extreme poverty does not prevent communisation; it will impose different communising ways.

To highlight that scarcity/abundance is not the major issue, we could suggest that communisation might prove more difficult to attain in what now passes as abundance. Food production is now quite far from modern cities, sometimes thousands of miles afar, and huge conurbations like London have moved wholesale markets to the suburbs or even further. Supermarkets as well as chain retail shops have their products brought to them by long distance transport, most of which relies on petrol. Whatever solutions will be found, they will depend on how the insurrection proceeds. For instance, if lots of people leave the city, it will not be just because town vegetable gardens are unable to feed millions: going to the country will be part of a new way of socialising. Basic "needs" will be the prime mover of communisation in neither London nor Sao Paulo.

§ 5: A World without Money?

The reader might be surprised that such a major topic should come *only now* in this chapter, but money could not be a starting point of our analysis. Only now, after exploring the transformation of work into activity, is it possible to see how communisation would do away with money.

Money expresses and materialises—even when virtual—a social relation based on value, which results from the existence of work as production for productivity (i.e., production based on time-count), on the search for minimum input to get maximum output, which takes us back to the social division of labour between worker and nonworker, which itself takes us back to the division of property between those with a hold over the means of production and those without, the former hiring the latter. The development of the market is a consequence, not the cause, of this social division of labour, and money a consequence of the progress of the market. The market is the meeting place where private independent producers compare and exchange. Therefore, if we tried to abolish the market but kept time-count (= value count), nothing would change.

Though value becomes "visible," reveals its existence in exchange, and in most societies for the last millennia in money exchange, value (hence money) is created by work as we have tried to define it. This is what has to be changed.

Today, free access, hard discount or special offers, especially in crisis times, cause stockpiling or overconsumption, because people feel a fear of want, fear of lacking food or essential items (a mobile phone is now a family and job imperative). Possessing lots of tins and bags of rice in my own home is a guarantee that I will not starve. To afford them and to be able to buy more next week, I need money. Money means safety for my family and myself. A regular income is money in the bank. Hoarding goes with property, and property is a border and a protection, a necessity of present life: unless one possesses an income, a flat, savings, an insurance policy, a family and a partner, one is outside society. Without belongings, you don't belong.

Insurrection tends to create a situation where no one fears to be excluded.

This (logical) fear of want will wither when communisation puts an end to property. Not to substitute *collective* to private property but to abolish all property, in the sense that everyone will have free access to living conditions, which includes the means of "production" and "consumption."

Communising is not making everything available to everyone without anyone paying, as if we merely freed instruments of production and modes of consumption from their commodity form: shopping made easy . . . without a purse or a Visa card.

The existence of money is often explained by the (sad, alas inevitable) need of having a means of distributing items that are too scarce to be handed out free: a bottle of Champagne has to have a price tag because there is little Champagne produced.

On the other hand, much is made of things reputed to "cost nothing" nowadays, like downloaded online songs, and well-meaning people ask for these to be available free. This neglects that free (or hacked) access exists because it parallels a huge pay market (*Yesterday* by Marianne Faithfull: £ 0.79). In a store, although millions of junk food products are manufactured every day, unless I pay £ 0.80 for a bag of crisps, I'll have to watch out for the security guard. Money is not something necessary to regulate the distribution of "costly" items (a house), and then unnecessary when it comes to distributing simple stuff (a DVD).

Money is not an unpleasant yet indispensable instrument: it materialises the way activities relate to one another, and human beings to one another.

Superficial critics denounce finance and praise what is known as the "real" economy, but the reality of a bed or a bag only becomes effective, and the object can have some *use* because it is treated (and acted upon) according to its cost in money terms—ultimately to the labour time incorporated in it. Nothing now seriously exists apart from its cost. It is unthinkable for parents who have a son and daughter to buy a car as birthday present for her and a cap for him. If they do, everyone will measure their love for their two children according to the respective amount of money spent on each of them. In today's world, for objects, acts, talents and people to exist socially, they have to be compared, reduced to a substance that is both common and quantifiable.

The duality of *use value* and *exchange value* was born out of a situation where each activity (and the object resulting from it) ceased to be experienced and appreciated for what it specifically is, be it bread or a jar. From then on, that loaf of bread and that jar existed above all through their ability to be exchanged for each other, and were treated on the basis of what they had in common: in spite of their different concrete natures and uses, both were comparable results of the same practice, labour in general, or abstract labour, liable to be reduced to a universal and quantifiable element, the average human effort necessary to produce that bread and that jar. Activity was turned into work. Money is crystallised labour: it gives a material form to that common substance.

Communisation will not abolish *exchange value* while keeping *use value*, because one complements the other.

In quite a few past uprisings, in the Paris Commune or in October 1917, permanent armed fighters were *paid* as soldiers of the revolution, which is what they were.

From the early hours and days of a future communist revolution, the participants will neither need, use nor receive money to fight or to feed themselves, because goods will not be reduced to a quantum of something comparable to another quantum. Circulation will be based on the fact that each action and person is specific and does not need to be measured to another in order to exist.

When building a house, there is a difference between making sure the builders will not be short of bricks and mortar (which we can safely assume communist builders will care about) and budgeting a house plan (which in present society is a prior condition). Communisation will be our getting used to counting *physical realities* without resorting to accountancy. The pen and pencil (possibly the computer) of the bricklayer are not the same as the double-entry book of the accounts department. The communisers' main concern will not be: How many bricks for the walls? But: *What kind of habitat shall we have? What kind of life?*

Capitalism will naturally (i.e. according to its supple and generative abilities) counteract the communising effort to get rid of money, by promoting alternative money, barter, black markets, and other alternatives (see below § 13).

§ 6: Parasitic Activities?

I once was in a small-town public library reading room, writing a letter to an American friend, when I felt like taking a look around. A couple of teenage girls were doing their homework. An old man was reading a news magazine. A woman in her thirties, probably a professional historian, had asked for a bound collection of papers from the library vault and was taking notes. Rather the activities that communists, anarchists, or simply humanists would approve of: becoming familiar with the printed word (this was before laptops), peaceful learning, self-enlightenment . . . the exact opposite from the ugly world of money-grabbing and war-making. Books Not Bombs! Then I wondered what exactly these people were doing. Homework certainly enlightens and contributes to what school does: reproducing this society: one of those girls might become a trader or soldier. Research is fine and also reproduces the university machine: *Publish or perish!* And out of all magazines and papers on the market, how many would a communist, anarchist, or humanist recommend reading? So I wrote to this American friend: *There are too many words in the world.* I thought I was being witty. Sometime later, she replied: *I would say there are too many cars.* She was right of course, except nowadays words are more and more manufactured, sold, bought, and consumed like cars. School, media, and academia words. True, censoring, bowdlerising, or burning books has always been a synonym for oppression. But nowadays, in democratic countries at least, it is the increasing overload of words and pictures that stands in the way of our enlightenment, not a deficiency of written, spoken, or screened information.

Parasitism is not only situated where it is blatant. The problem with school, for instance, is not just that it instils conservative ideas and habits. (In fact modern advanced education claims to teach the young how not to be sexist, colour-prejudiced, xenophobic, homophobic, etc.) It does inculcate bourgeois—or rather capitalist—ideology, but its basic function is to train the young for their future role in a class society dominated by work. The split between learning and doing, the obligation to sit in a classroom for fifteen years or more, and the evolution of teaching into an overpowering institution and business, all this has to do with the existence of work as a cut-off time-space required to be more and more productive. Communisers will only get rid of one separation by disposing of the other: they will change school by overthrowing our ways of production and everything that goes with them.

Likewise, the way the insurgents will "communicate" will determine the evolution of "information" habits and means. Since communisation ends all separations, it will not just get rid of *The Sun* to have a self-managed *Guardian*, on the "We Are the Media" principle. The problem with the media is not that they lie (they often tell the truth, or a truth) or are in the pay of big business (which most of them are). It is to be what they are: mediations connecting people who need (re)connection. It is the passive life we live, centred on wage-labour, and the consumption that comes with it, that force us to be mediated in order to relate to the world, and force us to fulfil an over-whelming desire to access instant information on everything and anything. McLuhan was no Marxist or Situationist, but his 1964 statement "the medium is the message" still carries weight. The very notion of *information* is a historical reality and category, which paralleled the ascension of the bourgeoisie and the rise of public opinion: it implies supposedly neutral facts detached from interpretation, as illustrated in the English and American press tradition of displaying news and comment on different pages. The public debating sphere based on genuine information was essential to the making of parliamentary democracy.

What might become of papers, radio, TV, and the internet, nobody can tell, but we can be sure that today's compulsion-obsession about information, its storage and obsolescence is related to the domination of value and *time* over our lives. An insurrectionary process will invent new means of personal and collective communication.

§ 7: Too Late to Save the Planet?

There's no intrinsic reason why a social system should care more about bees or the ice cap than about the well-being or health of the humans under its rule. Mere logic and ethics have little relevance here. Capitalism escalates into an increasingly intensive exploitation of natural resources, uses up million-year-old coal and oil in a couple of centuries, taps the water table without renewing it, impoverishes the soil and then improves it with fertilisers that further deplete it but later enriches it with more chemicals. This system constantly remedies the imbalance it generates by roundabout means that cause new imbalances that are remedied by more technology . . .

. . . and if need be by ideology: capitalism now preaches the gospel of sustainable development. It still forces upon us the deal it has prospered on since the Industrial Revolution: "Work hard today, so tomorrow you can enjoy the fruits of cornucopia." But it adds the rider: "Consume differently today, otherwise tomorrow your children will be in danger" (*differently* meaning: consume what you are now being sold).

The insurgents will not address ecological issues because—unlike today's foolish consumers—they would deny themselves out-of-season strawberries for the planet's sake and switch from cars to bikes in order to save biodiversity. It is the logic of protracted insurrection that breaks with hyperproduction and overconsumption: why would the insurgents need to develop more huge steel mills, cement works, or oil refineries? Managing them would be incompatible with what they will be doing. The move from *work* to *activity* rules out the possibility of a productivist continuation.

Agribusiness, for example, is directly connected to how we now move things and people (biofuels) and how we eat. As the capitalist way of life spreads planet-wide, so does environmently destructive livestock and factory farming. Communisers will not deal with it by deciding to substitute soya bean steak for red meat merely for nature's or the future's sake. They will not have to be (or be taught to become) virtuous, reasonable, and willing to master their desires in order to follow sound dietary rules. Change will result as much from spontaneous interaction as from decisions properly speaking. As it is unlikely that casual labourers will continue to toil in the Californian or Andalusian fields, the impulse to eat strawberries or green pepper any day of year in New York or Berlin will have to decrease. Similarly, as many overexploited meat-processing workers will leave their factories, this will have more impact on eating habits than decades of vegan campaigning.

About a century ago, chestnuts were the staple food of some rural areas of the French Central Massif. Such a "poor" diet does not compare favourably with the variety we have been accustomed to in "rich" countries. Who knows, we might well enjoy a more limited range of dishes than the abundance currently sold in the supermarket.

We have no planet-saving plan. In fact, one ought to be wary of any well-thought-out scheme, complete with charts and figures, purporting to prove the right method to stop global temperature from increasing by 2050. All we know is that there is an intimate connection between getting rid of the money world and value system based on wage-labour, and dismantling the industrial behemoth.

§ 8: Daily Life Changes or Big Issues?

> You cannot make the revolution.
> You can only be the revolution.
> —*The Dispossessed*, 1974

The trouble with philosophers, Polish novelist Witold Gombrowicz once suggested, is that they do not care about trousers and telephones. That remark did not apply to Nietzsche, who was hardly a communist but refused "to treat as frivolous all the things about life that deserve to be taken very seriously—nutrition, residence, spiritual diet, treatment of the sick, cleanliness, weather!" (*Ecce Homo*, 1888). It is everyday life we will change: cooking, eating, travelling, meeting people, staying on our own, reading, doing nothing, having and bringing up children, debating over our present and future, and this means we give daily life its fullest meaning. Sadly, since the phrase became fashionable in the late 1960s, "everyday life" has been usually limited to the out-of-work time-space, as if people gave up hope of altering the economy and wage-labour, and were contented with altering acts and doings of a lesser kind: feelings, body, family, sex, couple, food, leisure, culture, friendship.

On the contrary, communisation will treat the minor facts of existence for what they are: a reflection and a manifestation of "big" facts: money, wage-labour, companies as separate units and value accumulation centres, work-time cut off from the rest of our time, profit-oriented production, obsolescence-induced consumption, agencies acting as mediators in social life and conflicts, speeded-up maximum circulation of everything and everyone . . .

The capital-labour relation structures and reproduces society, and the abolition of this relation is the prime condition of the rest. But we would be foolish to wait for the *complete* disappearance of the company system, of money and the profit motive, before starting to change schooling and housing. Communisers won't be parochial, but acting locally will contribute to the whole change.

For instance, communising implies transforming our addiction to mediation and mediators. I was surprised some time ago to hear of the existence of *community organisers*. I shouldn't have been: present communities can't do without managing. A future society where people would feel a constant need for psychologists, therapists, enablers, and healers would prove its failure at building a commonwealth: we would still be incapable of addressing tensions by the flow of social interplay, since we would want conflicts solved by professionals.

Communisation will undo repressive (and self-repressive) institutions and habits, as well as create nonmercantile links which will tend to be more and more irreversible: "Beyond a certain point, one cannot come back. That tipping-point we must reach." (Kafka)

Making, circulating, and using goods without money includes breaking down the wall of a private park for the children to play, or planting a vegetable garden in the town centre. It also implies doing away with the split between the asphalt jungle cityscape and a natural world which is now turned into show, leisure places and theme parks, where the (mild) hardships of a ten-day desert trek make up for the aggravating compulsory Saturday drive to a crowded supermarket. It means practising in a social relation what has now to be private and paid for.

Communism is an *anthropological revolution* in the sense that it deals with what Marcel Mauss (hardly a revolutionary) analysed in *The Gift* (1923): an ability to give, receive and reciprocate. It means no longer treating our next-door neighbour as a stranger, but also no longer regarding the tree down the road as a piece of scenery taken care of by council workers. Communisation is the production of a different relation to others and with oneself, where solidarity is born not out of a moral duty exterior to us, rather out of practical acts and interrelations.

Among other things, as we said in § 6 about school, communisation will be the withering away of systematic distinction between *learning* and *doing*. We are not saying that ignorance is bliss, or that a few weeks of thorough (self-)teaching are enough for anyone to be able to translate Arabic into English or to play the harpsichord. Though learning can be fun, it often involves long hard work. What communism will do away with is the locking up of youth in classrooms. Actually, modern school tries to bridge the gap by multiplying out-of-school activities and work experience schemes. These remedies have little effect: the rift between school and the rest of society depends on another separation, which is structural to capitalism: the separation between work (i.e., paid and productive labour), and what happens outside the workplace and is treated as nonwork (housework, bringing up children, learning, leisure, and other things that are unpaid). Only superseding work as a separate time-space will transform the whole learning process.

In contrast to most utopias as well as to modern totalitarian regimes, communisation will not promote a "brave new world" full of *new (wo)men*, each equal in talents and in achievements to their fellow beings, able to master all fields of knowledge from Renaissance paintings to astrophysics, and whose own desires would always finally merge in harmony with the desires of other equally amiable fellow beings. A mistaken belief in Paradise is a sure way of accepting Hell . . . or lingering in Purgatory. Communisation is more straightforward:

As mass work stoppages and riots break with automatic social reproduction, they will create a suspension of disbelief of the proletarians *in themselves*, which will push them to invent something else *and themselves*. Individual and collective innovation will not be directly related to each participant's previous role. The bus driver will not be the one who decides what to do with buses. For a while, it will matter that she used to be the person behind the wheel: she knows better how to drive and maintain this vehicle. Only in that sense will professional skill play a specific provisional part. Then sociological determination will gradually become less important, and the essential will be whether we need or want buses, what sort, and to go where?

Some areas will lag behind and others may plunge into temporary chaos. Let us not expect the move to be smooth and tranquil everywhere and all the time.

> *Transform the world*, said Marx, *change life*, said Rimbaud; for us these two watchwords are one.
> —André Breton, "Speech to the Congress of Writers," Paris, 1935

§ 9: From Worker to After-Dinner Critic?

"For as soon as the distribution of labour comes into being, each man has a particular, exclusive sphere of activity, which is forced upon him and from which he cannot escape. He is a hunter, a fisherman, a herdsman, or a critical critic, and must remain so if he does not want to lose his means of livelihood; while in communist society, where nobody has one exclusive sphere of activity but each can become accomplished in any branch he wishes, society regulates the general production and thus makes it possible for me to do one thing today and another tomorrow, to hunt in the morning, fish in the afternoon, rear cattle in the evening, criticise after dinner, just as I have a mind, without ever becoming hunter, fisherman, herdsman or critic." (*German Ideology*, Part I, A)

This statement has been ridiculed by bourgeois for its naivety, and attacked by radicals for its acceptance of objectionable activities, hunting in particular, more generally its endorsement of humankind's domination over animals. Another critical view might ask why Marx reserves philosophy or art for the evening, as an afterthought, as if there was no time for it while producing food, which seems to take up most of the day in Marx's vision . . .

In 1845, Marx was providing no layout for the future, and he inserted his prejudices and preconceptions of his time. But *so do we today*, and we would be pretentious to think ourselves devoid of prejudices.

The most valid aspect of that statement remains the idea that people living in a communist world would not be tied to a trade or function for life, which still remains the fate of most of us. When this is not the case, mobility is often forced upon us: the least skilled usually get the worst jobs, the poorest pay, and lowest social image, and they are the first to be laid off and pressured into a retraining scheme. And as many of us have experienced, "multitasking" is a way of increasing labour productivity.

Work is class, and when a class society bothers to justify itself, it presents the *social* division of labour as a necessary and beneficial *technical* division: no one is able or willing to do a bit of everything, so everybody has to specialise, and the more developed society is, the more varied jobs there are. Unfortunately, some people have more brains or skills than others, so Sheryl works as a manager and Maria as a cleaner. Fortunately, if she is nimble in climbing the ladder, Maria is given the possibility of upward social mobility (if not, her children).

A frequent far-left answer to hierarchy is to fight for a world where everybody would do a bit of everything: Sheryl and Maria would both manage *and* clean. This is missing the point. Specialisation is more effect than cause. Work is done by masses at the bottom controlled by a few at the top, because work is separated from the rest of life, because we have no control over our lives: (re)appropriating them will do away at the same time with the division of our existence between work/nonwork, and with the division of labour.

As long as *work* exists *as such*, as a time-space reserved for production (and earning money), a hierarchy of skills will remain. Only the opening-up of productive acts to the rest of life will change the situation. Among other things, this implies the end of the present workplace as a specific distinct place, where only those involved in work are allowed in.

Let's take the example of an occupied printing plant in an insurrectionary area, with a labour force of fifty. If these fifty persons print leaflets, posters, and pamphlets for the cause but remain in charge of the tasks, and insist on the premises being off-limits for the neighbourhood people, they merely "serve" the movement. No money is being circulated, and they are not trying to be competitive, but their activity remains separate and the printing plant remains a separate production unit.

On the contrary, if the plant opens up onto the neighbourhood, not as a mere one-off Open Day but with the purpose of training former "outsiders" and systematically exchanging knowledge, if the printers start learning new trades, if the gap between "manual" and "intellectual" narrows, if raw materials are obtained without money or credit, if printed stuff circulates without being sold, if these nonmercantile links develop into networks that expand and come in conflict with State power, this diverse yet converging process contributes to communising society.

The autonomy that was necessary for the transformation to start has not vanished, but it is now of a totally different nature. Originally, on these premises, the *auto*, the *self* involved was the printers' workforce: they were the ones who first collectively stopped work. The difference is that, though none of though the fifty occupiers have not lost their skill, they are not *printers* anymore. Most of the time, each of them is also involved in something else. They often leave the place and the area to take part in demos, meetings, debates, or riots. While on the premises, they train people from the neighbourhood or from afar: someone who was just a plumber, a schoolteacher, or a hairdresser gets acquainted with the printing press. On the other hand, a photo-engraving specialist spends most days renovating a house. Work is not abolished like a republic abolishes monarchy: it is broken up into a potentially infinite series of moments and deeds that explode its time-space frame.

In our society, workers tend to be confined within a compartmentalised function, their technical skills are geared to the equally specialised machine they use, and the "service economy" makes it worse. One can know little about biology and be hired as a lab technician: the knowledge is in the software. The disruption caused by insurrection may turn out to be a blessing in disguise: it will help broaden the scope of our interests and abilities.

As with bus-driving, the "time factor" is not to be denied: there is a world of difference between Gutenberg's press, techniques that were new in the 1970s, and computer-aided printing (taking into account that a return to the "Prince of Presses" Original Heidelberg will have its enthusiasts). What matters is the social dynamics, with enough innovative energy to keep upping the ante and continually surpassing our own limits.

Revolution is not an inter-enterprise affair. Whatever name they choose, communising committees or collectives will not be trade- or work-based but territorial. Without the breaking up of work, and of the workplace, it would be impossible for instance to close (temporarily or for good) the printing plant, if it is a health hazard, or simply because the population thinks it has better things to do.

§ 10: What about Gender?

This theme could provide enough material for a whole book. Instead, we shall start with a tale that will stretch the imagination without losing credibility. Picture a large town insurrection, lots of people have stopped work, buses blocking the streets since dawn, tear gas at midday, discussions going on, now the time is 4:00 P.M. One by one, or in small groups or pairs, most women in their twenties and thirties leave the meetings and the occupied public buildings. Why? A majority of teachers are on strike and they've looked after young children all day, but it's school closing time and kids must be taken care of. So mothers are going to pick up their daughters and sons from school and prepare tea for them.

This is less of a sad joke than it seems. In many a big unrest or insurrection, masculine domination prevailed and still does, if not on the first afternoon as I have caricatured it but pretty soon afterward. Friends who took part in the 1960–61 Belgian general strike recall how intense the solidarity was, but it was always the women who would cook for the strikers and demonstrators. It is as if popular or worker revolts do not mind the subordination of women.[5]

The way communisation will ensure its own reproduction—and the reproduction of its members—will determine its future.

The man/woman relation is part of the whole social reproduction, but the division of labour (as seen in the previous section) is not sufficient to explain the *sexual* division of labour.

What is capitalism's novelty regarding man and woman?

Not that women work. They did before, on farms and in shops, but usually under the supervision of a husband: family coincided with the basic most common economic unit. Patriarchy was the rule of the heads of the household. The change came after women went into wage-labour. The process started with the Industrial Revolution, and it is significant that one of the first assertions of women's rights happened in England.[6]

Capitalism promotes sexual division and oppression, but patriarchy is not indispensable to it.

The continuation of masculine domination is neither a remnant of the past (though tradition has a part in it), nor just an effect of the policy of "Divide and Rule" which is a constant of any ruling class (though this also plays its part).

The specific unequal status for women is linked to social reproduction and the family.[7]

It is intriguing to see how communists envisaged the family in the middle of the nineteenth century:

> The bourgeoisie has torn away from the family its sentimental veil, and has reduced the family relation to a mere money relation. . . . The bourgeois claptrap about the family and education, about the hallowed correlation of parents and child, becomes all the more disgusting, as through modern industry, all the family ties among the proletarians are torn asunder, and their children transformed into mere articles of commerce and instruments of labour. . . . The bourgeois sees his wife as a mere instrument of production. . . . He has not even a suspicion that the real point aimed at is to do away with the status of women as mere instruments of production. (*Communist Manifesto*, chapters 1 and 2)[8]

Marx was right to refer the issue to production and reproduction. More than 150 years later, that situation has not ended: it's been extended to everyone. Man, woman, or child, we all are present, future, or potential "instruments of production."

Marx was wrong when he perceived the family as evolving into *a mere money relation*. It is and means a lot more. In a very different way from 1848, the family soldiers on, among bourgeois and proletarians, even in the most advanced capitalist societies, even more so in times of crisis when it provides the deprived with a protection they would rarely find elsewhere. This nonmercantile refuge is even more precious because it is eroded by money relationships and threatened in its role as a last resort against the "icy waters of egotistical calculation."

Paradoxically, the deeper social crisis goes, the more people ask from family bonds, the more contradictions the family has to bear, yet the more indispensable it is.

We do not live in Huxley's *Brave New World* (1932), which did away with natural reproduction, having children not be born but created, raised in "hatcheries," and later "conditioned."

Still, if children are still made and reared within the family, this raises the question of why the family is what it is. Why is it not developing into a fair, equal gender relation matrix, instead of remaining the main locus of the formation of sex roles and masculine domination? There is no simple answer. The prime reason is the maintenance of private property.

In our society, the pivotal role of private property goes far beyond the obvious fact that one cannot drive a car he does not own or has not bought access to, or has not been granted the use by the legitimate owner. This is what bourgeois ideology wants us to believe, that we all own a little something, and "there's nothing more despicable than a thief." The adjective *bourgeois* is no jargon, it is perfectly adequate here. The bourgeois are the proprietors of the essential (the means of production, i.e., the means of livelihood of the immense majority), and there is an ocean of difference between being a Toyota 5 percent shareholder and owning a flat where one lives. A better word for that difference is *class*. We do not live in an atomised world of individuals born out of nowhere: *family is a guardian and transmitter of private property*. Of course, members of most families die without bequeathing anything of value. That does not negate the key position of the family unit in the property system, and this role is made more complex but not nullified by the increasing number of divorces, stepfamilies, civil partnerships, and non-heterosexual families: it is natural that the legal right to inheriting money and assets should be one of the big stakes in civil partnerships and homosexual marriages.[9]

If private property disappears, what role is left for the family—the family as we know it, as it has existed for millennia as the bearer of a patrimony (the word is telling, like patriotism: what belongs to a father or a community of fathers)?

To return to our little tale, not only are women active in (and often initiate) protests and strikes, in the textile industry for instance from nineteenth-century England to contemporary Asia, but they do not back away from violent or armed action when they think it necessary. Let's just give two very different examples.

Mika and Hippolyte Etchebéhère came from Argentina to Europe in 1931 and joined the POUM, Hippolyte leading one of the POUM militias in 1936. When he was killed, Mika became *captain* of the militia which fought on the front lines of various battles.

From the late 1970s to the mid-1990s, the German all-woman group Rote Zora organised a series of symbolic bombings against such targets as the Federal Constitutional Court, big business or sex shops, managed neither to kill nor get killed, and the only member that was ever arrested received a suspended sentence.[10]

In spite of these examples and a thousand more, the involvement of women in radical action is not enough to counterbalance general masculine domination. Would the POUM militia members have accepted Mika if she had not been the deceased leader's widow? It all works as if, when men and women are concerned, fighting alongside and comradeship are not enough to result in "equality." An (anti)revolutionary division of labour takes place: women find themselves in charge of "female" affairs like cooking, nursing, and child minding. In struggles over housing, they tend to specialise in shopping, heating, food, or rent. Diversity and parity have little to do with it. Even a 50/50 mix on the barricade is no sign of how roles and identities will assert themselves a couple of days later.

It is not a question of sex proportion but of what the insurgents *do*.

It is the persistence of the duality of "public"/"private" spheres that ultimately takes women back to a "woman" role (i.e., a *family* role). An insurrection that cuts deep against work as such, against the economy, is bound to disrupt the continuation of these spheres. Disassembling the public/private duality is the condition for those women with talent for guns to stay on the street instead of taking the kids home, and for men with strong disposition for cooking to follow their inclination, until roles fluctuate. In the Belgian strike we referred to, woman participants were acting as proletarians' wives: in communist insurrection, women will take part as woman proletarians. We will only get rid of *work* and of the *family* at the same time.

A little of this happened in the 1970s in Italy, a little again on some of the Occupy sites.

On the other hand, as long as a movement remains within the confines of labour/capital bargaining or of democratic demands, even by violent means, women will not do much more than men and eventually get back to a "woman's place": the home, in one form or other. It is not a question of having thousands of Mikas instead of one, but of having a situation different from Spain in 1936. It was because women and men did *not* set communisation in motion that the subordination of women soon returned: the forced exclusion of women from the militias paralleled the forced incorporation of the militias into the bourgeois Republican army.

> That the abolition of individual economy is inseparable
> from the abolition of the family is self-evident.
> —*German Ideology*, Part I, A

Masculine domination will not wither in a day or month. The process will involve as much man/woman conflicts as tensions between radical/reformist (man and woman) proletarians in general. The *piqueteros* gave examples of the necessity and difficulty of solving such conflicts. But if this type of contradiction got the upper hand over the capitalism/communism contradiction, it would be a bad omen.

Capitalism is not the cause of women's subjugation, which predated capitalism by a few millennia and exists in societies nobody would qualify as capitalist. Yet today it is capitalism that perpetuates this subjugation, and we cannot fight it in general, only in its capitalist form shaped by wage-labour and private property. Revolution will not be caused by nor be moved forward by the contradiction between sexes, but it will only succeed if it addresses this contradiction.

§ 11: What about Violence?[11]

Up to now, rebels have usually brought the State to a standstill, and then either the State has crushed the uprising or the insurgents have let politicians curtail the insurrection by channelling its energy into institutions.

Communisation means that revolution will not be a succession of phases: first the dismantling of State power, social change afterward. This does not mean that it would be purely or mainly social and therefore apolitical or only marginally political. Communisation implies fighting public—as well as private—organs of repression. It is violent. (By the way, what democratic revolution ever won merely by peaceful methods?)

The difference with previous revolutions is that communisation proceeds far more by subversion than by elimination: it saps counterrevolutionary forces by removing their support. Communisers' propulsive force will not come from shooting capitalists but by depriving them of their function and power. Communisers will not target enemies but undermine social relations. The development of moneyless and profitless relations will ripple through the whole of society and act as power enhancers that widen the fault lines between the State and growing sections of the population. Our success will ultimately depend on the ability of our human community to be socially expansive.

Social relations, however, are incarnated in buildings, in objects, in institutions, in beings of flesh and blood, and historical change is neither instantaneous nor automatic. Some obstacles will have to be swept away: not just exposed but done away with. We will need more than civil disobedience: passive resistance is not enough. People have to take a stand, some will take sides against communisation, and a trial of strength does not just battle with words. The idea that our violence would be purely *defensive* is akin to believing in nonviolent violence. States (dictatorial or democratic) are enormous concentrations of armed power. When this armed power is unleashed against us, the greater the insurgents' fighting spirit, the more the balance of forces will shift away from State power, and the less bloodshed there will be.

An insurrectionary process does not just consist in occupying buildings, erecting barricades and firing guns one day, only to forget all about them the next. It implies more than mere spontaneity and ad hoc, ephemeral getting together. Unless there is some continuity, our movement will skyrocket today and fizzle out tomorrow. A number of insurgents will have to remain organised and available as armed groupings. (Besides, nobody has talents or desires for everything.) But if these groupings functioned as bodies specialised in armed struggle, they would develop a monopoly of socially legitimate violence, soon we would have a "proletarian" police force, together with a "proletarian government," a "people's army," etc. Revolution would be short-lived.

No doubt this will have to be dealt with in very concrete issues, such as what to do with police files we happen to find. Though revolution may exceptionally use existing police archives and security agency data, basically it will do away with them, as with all kinds of criminal records.

Revolution is not apolitical. It is *anti*-political:

Communisation includes the destruction of the State, and the creation of new administrative procedures, whatever forms they may take. Each dimension contributes to the other. None can succeed without the other. Either the two of them combine, or both fail. If the proletarians do not get rid of political parties, parliament, police bodies, the army, and so on, all the socialisations they will achieve, however far-reaching, will sooner or later be crushed, or will lose their impetus, as happened in Spain after 1936. On the other hand, if the *necessary* armed struggle against the police and army is only a military struggle, one front against another, and if the insurgents do not also take on the social bases of the State, they will only build up a counterarmy, before being defeated on the battlefield, as happened in Spain after 1936. If the idea was to outgun the State, only a would-be State would be up to it.

Here again, realists will advocate further industrial development, with special reference to the necessity of defending ourselves with state-of-the-art weaponry. Hi-tech arms production requires assembly lines, robotisation, process optimisation, management by experts, a security system within our ranks and a secret service to collect intelligence inside the enemy camp. There would be no other way: if you fight counterrevolution as an army opposed to another army, the aim is to have better organisation and equipment, and you do not manufacture drones in (nor operate them from) the village hall. This is what Lenin's party understood: it created a Red Army stronger than White armies. Bolshevik power won over bourgeois power.

Communisers will not beat the bureaucratic-military-industrial complex at its own game, only defeat it by playing their game.

Communist revolution does not separate its *means* from its *ends*.

Communisation can only happen in a society torn by mass work stoppages, huge street demos, widespread occupation of public buildings and workplaces, riots, insurgency attempts, a loss of control by the State over more and more groups of people and areas, in other words an upheaval powerful enough for social transformation to go deeper than a combination of piecemeal adjustments. Resisting anti-revolutionary armed bodies involves our ability to demoralise and neutralise them, *and* to fight back when they attack. As the momentum of communisation grows, it pushes its advantages, raises the stakes and resorts less and less to violence, but only a rose-tinted view can believe in bloodless major historical change.

At the Caracas World Social Forum in 2006, John Holloway declared: "The problem is not to abolish capitalism, but to stop creating it." This is indeed an aspect of communisation, summed up in *The Dispossessed*: our purpose is not so much *to make* as *to be* the revolution. Quite. But Holloway's theory of "changing the world without taking power" empties that process of any reality by denying its antagonism to the State. Like Holloway, we don't want to *take* power. But unlike him and his many followers, we know that State power will not wither away under the mere pressure of a million local collectives: it will never die a natural death. On the contrary, it is in its nature to mobilise all available resources to defend the existing order. Communisation will not leave State power aside: it will have to destroy it.

The Chartists' motto "Peacefully if we may, forcibly if we must" is right only in so far as we understand that we will be forced to act "forcibly."

How do we create a situation where no State is the "monopolist of violence," and where chaos does not reign? In revolutionary times, social violence and social inventiveness are inseparable: the capacity of the proletarians to control their own violence will depend on the ability of this violence to be as creative as destructive. For the destruction of the State to be more than an empty phrase, negative acts must also be positive—creative not of a new police, army, parliament, and so on but rather of new deliberative and administrative bodies that are directly dependent on social relationships.

§ 12: Who Would Be the Communisers?

"The proletarian movement is the independent movement of the immense majority, in the interests of that vast majority . . ." (*Communist Manifesto*). Both phrases are crucial: *independent movement* and *immense majority*. That being said, it does not follow that nearly everyone is a proletarian, nor that every proletarian can play the same part in the communising process. Some are more apt than others to initiate the change, which does not mean that they would be the "leaders" of the revolution. The exact opposite: they would succeed only in so far as they would gradually lose their specificity.

We do not live in a society where just about everybody is exploited and has the same basic interest in an overall change, therefore the same desire and ability to implement what would be a rather peaceful process because (nearly) everyone would join in: only 3 to 5 percent would object, Castoriadis assured us, but no doubt they would soon see the light.

We live neither in a post-industrial society, nor in a post-*class* society, nor therefore in a post–working class society. If work had become inessential, one might wonder why companies would have bothered in the last twenty years to turn hundreds of millions of Earthlings into assembly-line workers, crane operators, or computer clerks. Work is still central to our societies, and those in the world of work—currently employed or not—will have better social leverage power, at least in the early days or weeks of communisation.

This specific and (as we said before) provisional role would not turn them into a vanguard.

When railway workers are the only ones to go on strike, they are unlikely to look beyond their own condition: they simply do not have to. On the contrary, general strike, mass disorder, and rioting break the normal flow of social reproduction. The extension of work stoppages and of street and neighbourhood initiatives opens the possibility for railway personnel to move on to a different range of activities decided upon and organised by themselves *and* by others: for instance, instead of staying idle, they might be running trains—free, of course—to transport strikers or demonstrators from one town to another. It also means starting to think and act differently about the railway system, no longer believing in feats of engineering for progress's sake, and no longer sticking to the view that "high-speed trains are super because they're fast."

The success of communisation depends on the fading away of former sociological distinctions and hierarchies: breaching professional distances will go together with dismantling mental blocks regarding personal competence and aspiration. The process will be more complex than we expect, and more unpredictable: the experience of any large social movement (Germany 1918, Spain 1936, France 1968, Argentina 2001, to name a few) shows how volatile the unprecedented can be, when the situation slips out of control and creates both deadlocks *and breakthroughs*. One thing leads to another point of departure for further development. The railway example prompts the question of the fading of the difference between "public" and "private" transport, which in turn brings back the vital issue of where and how we live, since today's means of locomotion are conditioned by the urban segmentation of specific areas for administration, habitation, work, recreation, "nature," etc.

This is worth recalling in a time when, according to common radical opinion, the global downtrodden mass of human beings is endowed with the quiet force of progress strong enough to change the world: a mass so immense it encompasses no less than 99% of world population (even more than in Castoriadis's vision). This amounts to what plain language calls *the people*. The people does exist, it has repeatedly manifested itself throughout history, it is the 1848 democratic revolutions' people, more exactly before June 1848, before class reality asserted itself and the soldiers of the bourgeoisie shattered popular unanimity. It is the same *people* that appeared at the demise of bureaucratic regimes (in Poland, particularly), and recently in Arab countries and elsewhere.

In 2013, a Czech group made it clear they were not part of such a 99%, and provocatively wrote, *We Are the 1%*:

> You are the 99% who protest against the excesses of capitalism and the abuses of the State. You are the 99% who demand electoral reforms, social alternatives, economic aid, political measures. . . . We have never felt at home in 99% of our modern life, spent lining up to beg for crumbs, and yet you insist on defending 99% of the problem. We will take our possibilities elsewhere.[12]

The question is not *the personnel* of the revolution. There is an obvious difference between a university don and a supermarket cashier, but the point is what they can *do* and are likely to do together. If they merely get together, even with solidarity, mutual help, communal meals and child care, and do not break with market rule, there won't be a great deal of change.

§ 13: Reaching the Tipping Point?

How will we get to—and pass—the turning point Kafka was referring to?

Bourgeois strategy will be twofold: where it is unable to contain the rebellion, it will weather the storm, stall, sit out the events, and wait for insurgent energy to peter out; where it feels powerful enough, it will be proactive and break up unrest.

One of the main points all previous paragraphs tried to make is that creativity will be our strongest asset.

Against those who will want to keep money as a convenient instrument of measure, communism will come by creating a different life with no need for value. People will count in kilowatts and not in time, because their activity will have no use for a substance common to all tasks and objects.

This will not be achieved in a month, nor without resistance and confrontation with law and order forces. Sometimes communist endeavours will be repressed. Sometimes they will be deflected and deviated, because creativity functions both ways.

When money regresses but new ways of life are still unsure, all kinds of makeshift solutions come up, from barter, alternative currency and *time banks* . . . to the black market.

Social money reform schemes are not a credible alternative to capitalism as it exists, nor a way of seriously ameliorating it. Complementary currencies are what the term suggests: they make up for deficiencies. German towns introduced municipal currencies after 1918 to palliate the absence of a stable trustworthy Mark. In the depressed 1930s, in order to stimulate exchange, some Swiss and Austrians experimented special currencies valid within a group of firms and co-ops, or even *melting money*, which loses 1 percent of its value every month to discourage hoarding. Some of these schemes still exist as an inter-company barter mechanism. In the 1980s, Local Exchange

Trading Systems were born as a remedy to economic devitalisation, notably in Argentina, where barter clubs (often for out-of-work middle-class people) developed in the 1990s. Now Italian *time banks* admit time checks between people that owe each other time, and there exist semiofficial *time dollars*. With local money being only valid locally, the hope is to recreate a genuine community that evades finance control over healthy activities, by promoting forms of trade that serve solidarity and ecological purposes. So far Argentina is the only country where social currencies ever reached an economic national threshold, but the worsening of the present crisis is reviving expedients and palliatives that mitigate mass impoverishment. Instead of doing away with money, people make do with alternative money. Local economy *is* economy, and interpersonal time-count is value with a human face.[13]

Social inventiveness is indeed a revolutionary asset, yet periods of upheaval also generate nonrevolutionary projects and experiments. An oddity like bitcoin cryptocurrency, now a commercial and financial tool, may become a way of regulating exchanges when normal circuits are out of order. Though hardly viable in the long run, these interim solutions could help sidetrack the communist critique of wage-labour and work.

This is just an example of what lies in store for us. Revolution is fun and hard times—both. No short cut. No straight line. The Paris Commune has been called "the greatest festival of the nineteenth century," but revolution fails if it limits itself to a violent festival of the oppressed.

What we are running up against is not just riot police, it is formless and pervasive. If capitalism has the magnitude of a civilisation, where do its momentous drive and resilience come from? Undoubtedly from its amazing and always renewed capacity to invent advanced ways of exploiting labour, to raise productivity, to accumulate and circulate wealth. But also from its fluidity, its ability to supersede rigid forms, to remodel hierarchy and discard vested interests when it needs to, not forgetting its adaptability to the most varied doctrines and regimes. It is this unprecedented plasticity that gives capitalism the scope of a civilisation. It derives from the fact that it has no other motive than to create abstract value, to maximise its flow, and eventually to set in motion and accumulate more figures than goods.

Capitalist civilisation develops extreme individualism, while creating a *universality* of sorts, which is also a form of *freedom* (of which democracy is the political realisation): it breeds and favours a new type of human being potentially disconnected from the ties of tradition, land, birth, family, religion, and established creeds. In the twenty-first century, a modern Londoner eats a banana grown in the West Indies (where she was holidaying last week), watches an Argentine film, chats up an Australian woman on the internet, rents a Korean car, and from her living room accesses any classical or outrageously avant-garde work of art as well as all schools of thought. Capitalism is selling her no less than an infinite range of possibilities. Fool's gold, we might object, because it is made of passivity and spectacle in the Situationist sense, instead of truly lived-in experience. Indeed . . . Yet, however specious this feeling of empowerment, it socially "functions" as it is able to arouse emotion and even passion.

We would be wrong to assume that a period when communisation is possible and attempted would automatically and quickly eliminate the appeal of false riches—material or spiritual. Two centuries of modern capitalist evolution have taught us how resourceful that system can prove. In troubled times, social creativity will not only be on our side: in order to ride out the storm, capitalism also will put forward authenticity and collectiveness. It will provide the individual with opportunities to go beyond his atomised self. It will suggest critiques of "formal" democracy, defend planet Earth as a shared heritage, oppose cooperation to competition and use to appropriation. In short, it will pretend to change everything . . . except capital and wage-labour.

The communist perspective has always put forward an unlimited development of human potentials. Materially speaking: everyone should be able to enjoy all the fruits of the world.

But also in the "behavioural" field, in order to promote, harmonise and fulfil talents and desires against all upholders of the norm. The surrealists ("absolute freedom") and the Situationists ("to live without restraints") went even further and extolled the subversive merits of transgression.

Today, the most advanced forms of capitalism turn this critique back on us. Current political correctness and its Empire of Good leave ample room for provocation, for verbal and often factual transgression. Let us take a look at the many screens that surround us: compared to 1950, the boundary is increasingly blurred between what is sacred and profane, forbidden and allowed, private and public. English readers had to wait until 1960 to buy the unexpurgated version of *Lady Chatterley's Lover*. Henry Miller's *Tropic of Cancer*, published in Paris in 1934, was banned until 1961 in the United States, 1963 in Britain. Fifty years later, online pornography, whatever that questionable wording covers, is widespread (according to obviously unverifiable statistics, 12 percent of all sites and 25 percent of internet searches deal with pornography). Contemporary counterrevolution will appeal much less to moral order than it did in the 1920s and '30s, and often have a "liberal-libertarian" and permissive-transgressive flavour. Communisation, on the other hand, will prevail by giving birth to ways of life that tend to be universal but not dominated by addiction, virtuality, and public imagery.

§ 14: How Relevant Is This Questions and Answers List?

Have our successive sections "answered" the questions asked? Rather, they have posed new ones. This questionnaire is for the reader to ask more questions of her or his own.

At the risk of overstating our case, let's affirm that capitalism is neither self-animated value nor almighty merchandising: it is the forced union of capital and labour.

The last two hundred years are ample proof that *resisting* exploitation is no automatic one-way road to *doing away with* exploitation.

The problem of communist theory is not to try and prove that communisation is feasible because "communism can work." It is to wonder how resistance to exploitation and dispossession can achieve more than aggravating the crisis of the system and can destroy it once and for all.

The current crisis, like others before, illustrates this ambivalence. The proletarians play an active part in capital's predicament: by their resistance (even when there are defeated, as they often are) mainly in the West, and by their surge for demands, mainly in Asia. Everywhere labour reacts to capital. The question is how much the fundamental social contradiction (capital/wage-labour) contributes to radical critique.

For class struggle to do more than keep itself going, it is not enough that capital becomes incapable of hiring labour: two or three billion jobless will not take on capital *just because* they are out of stable employment. Proletarians have experienced thirty years of redundancies in the old metropolises. For what official figures are worth, in the European Union, twenty-six million people were jobless in 2013; in the United States twelve million, plus ten million part-timers looking for full-time jobs (altogether nearly 15 percent of the labour force). This has resulted in unrest but has hardly radicalised much in a communist sense.

Labour finds itself in a situation when it can begin a self-critique of work when workers move from one predicament to another, by alternating periods of employment and unemployment, contract and unofficial work, protected and casual jobs. This helps create a situation where different categories meet, as *started* to happen in Greece, 2008, where also "ethnic" barriers (national/foreign, Greek/Albanian) began to crumble. Anti-work attitudes are more likely to emerge when the proletarian is set off balance by an in-between situation: he is neither totally excluded (as in unemployed families from mother to daughter), nor totally sure of his job. The civil servant who is entirely caught *in* the world of work, and the permanent beggar entirely left *out* of it, may be part of a revolution, but they will probably not initiate a critique which also has to be a self-critique.

No decisive change occurs as long as production goes on . . . nor as long as producers stop work without doing anything more.

Revolutionary moment is when the insurrection interrupts social reproduction and pioneers something new: capitalism's "non-reproducibility" happens then and only then.

Insurrection creates conditions where fear of separation fades away. Private appropriation is the foundation of all separations: it cuts human beings from their means of existence, their lives, others, and themselves. Revolution reunites proletarians and means of production, proletarians, and nature.

Only communisation answers the fundamental revolutionary conundrum: How can class struggle bring about not just the victory of one class against another but a victory that is also the abolition of both? How can the proletariat "win" and self-destruct at the same time? Our theoretical "basis" is also our problem.

The solution is not to have more of the *same*: more struggles, more insurgents, more autonomy, more fighting spirit, more weapons: all these are necessary conditions but only by abolishing themselves as proletarians will the proletarians defeat the bourgeois.

"When the proletariat is victorious, it by no means becomes the absolute side of society, for it is victorious only by abolishing itself and its opposite." (Marx and Engels, *The Holy Family*, IV, 4, 1844)

As the reader who has gone this far knows by now, the running theme of this book is the simultaneous existence of two conflicting possibilities and attitudes contained in the proletarian experience, so it will come as no surprise that this chapter should end on an ambivalent quote:

"Well, well," said Dick, "what shall I do then?"

"Just remember," said Miss Goering, that a revolution won is an adult who must kill his childhood once and for all."

"I'll remember," said Dick, sneering a bit at Miss Goering.

—Jane Bowles, *Two Serious Ladies*, 1943[14]

CHAPTER 7

■ A VERITABLE SPLIT

§ 1: Polemics

> I never attack people,—I treat people as if they were high-
> intensity magnifying glasses that can illuminate a general,
> though insidious and barely noticeable, predicament.
> —Nietzsche, *Ecce Homo*, 1888

The taste for polemics is usually proportional to the inability to influence reality.

Nobody can be reproached for this inability, only for the habit of making up for it through verbal violence.

When we spot a flaw in a theory, either we don't care or we express disagreement. But whenever a theory really matters, it's because of its kernel of truth, however debatable its expression can be. So theoretical discussion means pointing to *the strong point* of what is at stake in the debate, Nietzsche's "general predicament." Political feuds do the exact opposite: they concentrate on the shortcomings of the opponent and fish out the most questionable quotes, because the aim is not to understand but to debunk.

Because of the situation described in chapters 4 and 5, because the various categories of proletarians find it difficult to merge into the insurrectionary critical mass that communist theory calls *the proletariat*, this difficulty results in fractured radical attitudes and views. There is now little connection between attacking the State and experimenting new ways of life, or between street action and workplace militancy. These discrepancies are reflected in a real intellectual split where each partial theory is supposedly validated when it refutes the partiality of the others. Only a revolutionary surge will bring together and transcend these now isolated dimensions.

§ 2: It Takes More Than a Step Aside

Call and *The Coming Insurrection* (first published in French in 2003 and 2007) have *communisation* as one of their guiding themes. As both books are readily available in English, summing them up is unnecessary, and we will start with one of their basic tenets: the premise that society has become a social desert. Consequently, if we all live in a no-life space-time, a reemerging real community can be subversive. Deserting the desert by "disaffiliation" is creating "foci of desertion, of secession poles, of rallying points" that build up "the world civil war": "we need places . . . to get organised, to share and develop the required techniques." (*Call*)

"On the one hand, we want to live communism; on the other, to spread anarchy."

"As we apprehend it, the process of instituting communism can only take the form of a collection of *acts of communisation*, of making common such-and-such space, such-and-such machine, such-and-such knowledge. That is to say, the elaboration of the act of sharing that attaches to them. Insurrection itself is just an accelerator, a decisive moment in the process." The aim is "the sharing or communising of what we have at our disposal." In that sense: "Communism is possible at every moment."

If "what one could at present understand by communisation [is] in short, how to realise the immediacy of social relations," the question is: when does this immediacy start? To press the point, *has communisation already started?*

A shift is noticeable between the two books, but the presupposition was all at the beginning. The type of action suggested by *Call* consisted mainly in interrupting flows, since capitalism was defined as existing more in circulation than in production. Four years later, *The Coming Insurrection* presented work and production as inessential: "capital had to sacrifice itself as a wage relation in order to impose itself as a social relation." This is the Italian *autonomia* thesis that work has lost its productive necessity (of objects as well as of value), and that capitalism maintains work as a means of social control. According to the Invisible Committee, wage-labour as a relation has disappeared: what we can act on is social space. As the catastrophe is already here and we live a nonlife, and as blocking production would be ineffective, we can still *sabotage* that social space by changing our submissive daily habits and making inroads into new ways of life.

These books share a common misleading vision: modern society would be all networks and no centre of gravity. Both books describe aspects of reality as if they all supported each other only because we accept them, as if nonacceptance was enough for the edifice to fall apart. *Work* is the blind spot of that mind-set. The Invisible Committee believes that those on the edge of wage-labour (living on welfare, minor theft, mutual help, getting by) are turning into the majority, like a margin taking over the whole page. When every labourer is out of work or casual, the wage-system breaks up. This is forgetting that however large the unemployed or semiemployed world population becomes, work still rules.

"Getting organised in order not to be forced to work." When? Right now, *The Coming Insurrection* says, because rupture in the fabric of social life is on its way, it's happening and growing, and we have to be part of it to push it further.

What does that mean exactly?

The Invisible Committee misinterprets multiple and multiplying acts of resistance for a rupture: this is a theory of violent but gradual passage to communism.

This is consistent with an epoch when social ties come unloose and we all long for the most possibly humane authentic "connection," preferably with a radical touch. I browse in bookshops in the afternoon and buy on Amazon at midnight. Even the biggest smartphone addict feels nostalgic after the death of a village café, corner store, or countryside pub, and we would like to believe that reviving community ties might improve our quality of life and (who knows? . . .) alter life altogether. *Call* and *The Coming Insurrection* genuinely ride this wave. If I can't beat supermarkets, at least I will buy locally produced organic fruit and vegetables, as the writer of this book and certainly its readers often do. The mistake is to make (wrong) theory out of it, and the ambiguity present in *Call* had not been cleared up four years later. On the contrary, *The Coming Insurrection* would have us believe that, providing we choose the right steps, structural change can be achieved step by step.

Equating communisation with alternativism matches the general prevailing mood of despair about revolution. Rejecting an October 17–style seizure of power is about the only lesson most of our contemporaries—many radicals included—have drawn from the past century. All they are left with is a belief that an inch-by-inch reformation of daily life would gradually involve more and more people and domains until quantity might develop into qualitative transformation. Social revolution is replaced by a million personal and microcollective revolutions. Needless to say, so many local *foci* would be overturned that State forces would find themselves powerless.

These two books are often read like *The Revolution of Everyday Life* adapted to the early twenty-first century. But despite its shortcomings, in 1967 Raoul Vaneigem's book advocated the advent of worker councils extended to the whole of society, and worker management enlarged to the managing of life, which meant a historic break. None of that with the Invisible Committee or its successors and followers. As the capitalism they portray is at the end of its tether, an "entity in agony" nearing "imminent collapse," only our inertia keeps it alive. We are its life-support machine: what we have to do is withdraw our support. Supposing we all stepped aside . . .

§ 3: Decoupling Proletarian from Worker

This section addresses the consensus originally shared by TC-SIC's various components, notwithstanding later disagreements and splits, which will be approached in the next section.[1]

3.1: The Two-Stage Postulate

For TC-SIC as for many other radical circles, including us, it was rereading Marx that started it all—or a lot of it. Rereading and reassessing.

Probably SIC-TC's fatal flaw was failing to situate where Marx is to be criticised, where he was the most tied to his time: his progressivist streak. There lies the real parting of ways between SIC-TC and us.

Progressivism is more than a belief in today being better than yesterday and tomorrow being better than today. It implies faith in an inevitable evolutionary course, where history is a succession of linear steps, each superior to the preceding one. The ascending bourgeoisie portrayed itself as the head of a process where each phase logically prepared the next which was bound to be more prosperous, more peaceful and fairer to all.

True, Marx kept denouncing bourgeois progress, which he said brought with it crisis, misery, and war. But he believed in the rise of a worker movement which the triumphant march of industrial capitalism fostered in spite of itself, like an unwanted child bound to murder his horrible father one day. The ascent of the proletariat paralleled bourgeois development. Communists partake of progressivism when they think that capitalism does not just create *the conditions* of revolutionary change but *makes* the change itself or at least leads to it. The difference can be quite subtle, and Marx often crossed the line between the two positions. He repeatedly tried to accelerate the course of events, to spur the wavering ruling class into fulfilling its historical role so that the proletariat could finally sound the death knell of a spent system.[2]

Marx saw capitalism as the historical epoch bound to give birth to socialism or communism *because of the productive forces it developed*, a logic that naturally went with the primacy of work and the working class.[3]

The Second and later Third International took up progressivism and added an ultimate step different from the bourgeois goal: history was unavoidably getting nearer to the point when the working class would make the revolution (in the radical version), or socialise capitalism (in the reformist version).

Even if TC-SIC's "stagist" view of history differs from Marx's, even if it understands communism and revolution in quite a different way, the postulate remains.

As evolved by TC-SIC, the two-stage theory is not the notion that capitalism has gone through a succession of phases, which is obvious. It is the theory that divides capitalist history into two completely distinct periods, each with a completely different connection between reform/revolution, worker/proletarian, worker movement/revolution: in the first period, reformist class action was inevitable; in the second, it becomes impossible. All of nineteenth-century capitalism and nearly all of twentieth-century capitalism is defined as a single epoch summed up by one feature—the self-assertion of the proletariat within capitalism, the affirmation of worker identity—the closure of which happened in the last decades of the twentieth century. TC-SIC says we are now living in an era when the capital-labour relationship can no longer reproduce itself.

Because Marxism held that capitalism had to run its course, it supported the (capitalist, what else?) development of productive forces, under bourgeois or bureaucratic command, on the grounds that this would ultimately bring about socialism or communism.

Though its goal is the exact opposite of Marxism (TC-SIC aims at communism, not capitalism), it still maintains a two-phase logic: up to yesterday a necessarily long capitalist phase, followed by inevitable revolution today.

TC-SIC's basic belief is that we are now reaching the highest possible stage, the one when social reproduction of the capital-labour relationship cannot go on. Says who? The theory is based on an assumption that itself needs proving:

3.2: What Worker Identity?

That concept holds centre stage in a vision which makes just about everything depend on *worker class identity* being available before, and unavailable now.

Of course identity is not taken in a psychological-sociological-behavioural sense, only in a social-historical one.[4]

Working-class identity combines three elements: (1) collective acts that create togetherness (resisting the boss, fighting the police when they side with the boss, and so on); (2) formal membership of a union, labour party, etc.; (3) an ideological sense of belonging ("class consciousness"). What about these today? Element 3 has declined a lot. Number 2 has declined less but a lot too. Element 1 is still going on: numerous acts of collective self-defence occur in the workplace and out of it. Differently from 1960, no doubt. But is there more of a *qualitative* difference between 1960 and 2018 than between 1900, 1930, 1960, and 2018?

No insurrection has attempted communisation as described in TC-SIC's writings and in this book: at least we can agree on that.

The question is what the workers' project was when insurgents had enough energy and time to try and implement it: in 1871, 1917, 1919, 1936 . . .

A short answer is: a workers' world, freeing labour from capital, developing mass production to satisfy basic needs and liberate time for leisure. As a Chinese communist said in the 1920s: The future world must be a workers' world. A bit like what the Spanish proletariat might have achieved if they had not been crushed by Franco and Stalin: a federation of democratic agriculture and industrial collectives.

This is too short an answer.

Insurgent workers rarely attempted to take over the factories and run them in the place of the bourgeois.

In troubled times, revolutionary or radical workers did not strive to install worker-led capitalism. They *resisted* work in the occupied Italian factories in 1920. In Russia, there was worker control in 1917 but little attempt at worker management afterward. Spain in 1936 also witnessed a large grassroots resistance to productive efforts.[5]

In less troubled times, there has been very little labour interest in *production* co-ops. Workers hardly ever try to take control of a firm that's doing fairly well. They only do so in the hope of saving their jobs when a company goes bust or the owner has fled, as happened on a mass scale in Portugal in 1974–75. Otherwise militant labour prefers to leave the bourgeois in charge. Every time unions or parties replaced the bourgeois for a while, as in the Austrian socialisations after 1918, or in a number of French firms after 1945, the rank and file let its leaders do it, showed little enthusiasm and behaved more or less as labour always does when put to work by managers.

Or are we to understand that "worker identity" is incarnated in the political programmes that call for a partly or totally worker-managed economy, programmes like those put forward by a powerful worker movement? In that case, let's remember that the pioneer and longtime leading industrialised country, Britain, only had a real Labour *party* and what could be called a "worker political perspective" after 1918. In what became the main capitalist country, the United States, big unions never put forward a *specific* political perspective, and the socialist party always remained on the fringe. In so far as Bernstein was representative of a large undercurrent, he did not stand for worker affirmation, rather for the opposite, the dissolution of worker identity in a growing middle class. It was only after 1945 that the German SPD and unions tried to co-run the economy: in 1918–19, at the peak of their power and with mass worker support, they left the bourgeois in charge, and no grassroots pressure was exerted on them to act otherwise.

How deep did the affirmation of the worker and work go? Though workerist ideology was common, the political perspective of a world truly led by labour as a class was a lot less frequent. Mainstream and influential unions hardly questioned the leadership of the bourgeois over the economy. Only *revolutionary syndicalism* fought for worker-led capitalism: before 1914, the French General Confederation of Labor (CGT), the Italian

Syndicalist Union (USI) founded in 1912, plus the English and American Socialist Labour (and Labor) Parties. In a different way, De Leon wanted political rule to be the direct emanation of organised labour: an All-Industrial Congress would effectively function as government. But *syndicalism*—different from trade unionism—was the product of the pre-Fordist era, it was on the wane before 1914 (in France as early as 1906), and soon declined after World War I. Inasmuch as the German Left was workerist, only a tiny minority of workers remained in the KAPD and the *Unionen* after 1921.[6]

To sum up, the workers have had a negative or passive attitude toward managing their own firm and the economy in general. The obstacle to revolution was not that labour could only fight for a worker-led capitalism (taking the place of the bourgeois), or more moderately for a joint worker-bourgeois management (Australian style in the first half of the twentieth century, Scandinavian later, German after 1945).[7] Even though no one would seriously deny the reality of mass reformism, this fact can hardly be explained solely by the thesis of "working-class affirmation as a class within capitalism."

The two-stage theory boils down to saying that the worker movement acted as the best enemy of the revolution (the best and worst because it was the enemy from within): *workers*, defined and self-defined by work (whether they had a job or wanted one) rarely acted as *proletarians* (reserve-less persons having only their chains to lose and ready to overthrow capital and wage-labour). Why? According to TC-SIC, because they had this work possibility and prospect, both immediate (getting a job and fitting into capitalist society) and as a perspective (the political programme of a world based on industry). Workers could never turn into proletarians, because they were caught in a job, the work ethic, a closed-in solidarity, and in crisis time the hope of saving *their* company or *their* country's economy.

This, we are told, was the past: capitalism in its terminal stage is putting an end to stable employment, company, craft, country . . . Rural disruption worldwide is depriving hundreds of millions of their means of livelihood while enabling only a few to obtain wage-labour, and even so they receive a pittance barely able to reproduce their labour power and support their family. Statistically there still are blue-collar workers (albeit fewer than before), but there is no room for a worker movement. Up to now, the proletarian was the negative of an always desperately positive reality, the working class: at last the entirely negative has arrived. The worker/proletarian dilemma is soluble in contemporary capitalism.

To substantiate itself, this thesis maintains that there is no social space any longer for reformism, no possibility left for labour to organise and press for demands.

Here again, the claim is not supported by facts. On a world scale, as we have briefly seen in chapter 5, labour is *still* getting organised and pressing for demands. Though Asian and Latin American (African to a much smaller extent) labour struggles are not all or only factory-focused, they are often directly or indirectly related to work.

Are all workers completely atomised or all already on the way to insurrection? Neither, of course. A lot of them are fighting, some rioting, getting organised in various autonomous or institutional forms, creating and leaving unions, sometimes not bothering with permanent formal gatherings, sometimes keeping the action within the confines of workplace or trade, sometimes rejecting these limits. Refusing to call this a *worker movement* is only possible if one decides to narrow its definition to the forms of the *Old* Labour Party, European social-democracy, the French, Italian, Spanish, or Portuguese CPs in their heyday, or the militant CIO of the 1930s. Of course this is gone. But these institutions, and the type of worker struggle and class identity that fostered these unions and parties, merely went on for a few decades: the worker movement existed before, it has taken new forms since. Its 1900 forms differed as much from the 1950 ones as the worker movement today differs from 1950.

Demonstrating the opposite is only possible if one believes that *work* has stopped being *central* to capitalism. It has not. By work I don't mean *jobs*. The undeniable fact that there are far fewer job offers than job-seekers on this planet does not negate the centrality of work as producer of (surplus) value which remains the lifeline of the present world. Therefore labour confronts capital. Capitalism and reformism will go together as long as capitalism exists.

TC-SIC's theory is wrong on both counts: on the past and on the present.

The Situationists once suggested we ought to "go back to a disillusioned study of the classic worker movement" (*Situationist International* 7, 1962). Indeed. To face up to our past, we must break with the legend of a proletariat invariably ready for revolution . . . and unfortunately sidetracked or betrayed. But we don't get rid of myths by bending the stick the other way, as if the workers had up to now persistently fought only for reforms, had glorified work, believed in industrial progress even more than the bourgeois, and dreamt of an impossible worker-run capitalism. This historical reconstruction replaces one myth by its equally misleading symmetrical opposite.

The sad thing is that such theorising obscures what is really at stake in the argument: revolution *cannot* be the result of a work-centred community of struggle in a capitalist world that *is* work-centred. Closed-in worker struggles create an inward-looking class experience (the "us v. them"[8]) that proletarians only go beyond in insurrection. Communist revolution has a relation with class confrontation, but is not a mere intensification of it. The proletarians have stumbled over this obstacle—and communist theory has grappled with it—for nearly two centuries.

Here is Marx's basic definition of the proletariat:

> a class with radical chains, a class of civil society which is not a class of civil society, an estate which is the dissolution of all estates, a sphere which has a universal character by its universal suffering and claims no particular right because no particular wrong, but wrong generally, is perpetuated against it; which can invoke no historical, but only human, title; . . . a sphere, finally, which cannot emancipate itself without emancipating itself from all other spheres

of society and thereby emancipating all other spheres of society, which, in a word, is the complete loss of man and hence can win itself only through the complete re-winning of man. (*A Contribution to the Critique of Hegel's Philosophy of Right*, Introduction, 1843)

TC-SIC turns this undoubtedly *contradictory* (a class which is not a class) definition, which Marx applied to the proletariat in general, into a phase, a historical stage, the one we live in now: we are supposedly entering the time when the proletariat is about to act as a class that can't be a class anymore. Alexander is said to have sliced in half the Gordian knot he could not untie. In history, this is impossible. On paper, with a stroke of the sword-pen, the "Alexandrian solution" works fairly well. In real life it is still up to the proles to untie the knot: namely unbind themselves through revolution.

3.3: The Great Simplifier

TC-SIC believes in two entirely separate phases: one when the proletariat fought to affirm itself as a class, one when it can't because capitalism does not allow it anymore. This amounts to a *final crisis* theory, with the indomitable merit of making everything simple:

Crisis is supposed to impoverish all proles, homogenise them, put an end to bourgeois divisive policies, level down society, create a polarisation between two extremes: a powerless ruling class made socially redundant against immense out-of-labour labour unified at last.

Slicing up history into phases is useful, except when it becomes a quest for the "last" phase.

In the past, "final" or "mortal crisis" theoreticians set out to demonstrate (usually with the help of the reproduction schemas of *Capital* volume II) that a phase would necessarily come when capitalism would be structurally unable to reproduce itself. All they actually showed was real fundamental contradictions but, as Marx wrote, contradiction does not mean impossibility. Nowadays the demonstration has moved away from schemas and figures, and sees the impossible reproduction in the capital-labour relation itself. In short, up to now, communist revolution (or a real attempt to make it) had been out of the question, because the domination of capital over society was not complete enough: there was some scope for the worker movement to develop socialist and Stalinist parties, unions, reformist policies; so the working class *had to* be reformist, and the most it could do was to go for a worker-managed capitalism. Now this would be over: capital's completely *real* domination destroys the possibility of anything but a communist endeavour.

We ought to be a bit wary of the lure of catastrophe theory. When 1914 broke out, and even more so after 1917, communists said that humankind was entering the epoch of wars and revolutions. Since then, we have seen a lot more wars than revolutions, and no communist revolution. And we are well aware of the traps of the "decadence" theory. All variations of the "ultimate crisis" look for a one-way street that could block the avenues branching off to noncommunist roads. Yet history is made of crossroads, revolution being one possibility among nonrevolutionary options. The schematisation of history loses its relevance when it heralds the endpoint of evolution—in this case, capitalist evolution—and claims to be the theory to end all theories.

The concept of communisation is important enough as it is, without using it to prove that we have entered an entirely new era when the proletariat can *only* fight for communism.

No watershed moment in the evolution of a system can be considered final before the system has ended.

"Otherwise the application of the theory to any period of history would be easier than the solution of a simple equation of the first degree." (Engels, letter to Joseph Bloch, September 21, 1890)

It's interesting to note how new historical slices are carved. We are told that communist revolution was impossible under nineteenth-century *formal* capitalist domination, yet *real* domination lorded over the twentieth century, with intense class struggle yet few attempts at communist revolution.[9] So theory cuts real domination into two and delineates a *second* real domination phase, more real than the first: this time, at long last, no dead-ends, no side roads: reformism and radical democracy become devoid of content, and unions and parties have lost their grip. If the ideas differ from usual "final crisis" theses, the method is similar: a search for the ultimate stage with only one alternative. No doubt, in twenty years, if revolution has not come, the same we've-explained-it-all theory will define a *third* phase within real domination.[10]

3.4: The Ratchet Effect

Nothing will force the proletarians to act as communisers. Communism comes to solve a historical problem, but the solution implies a will to give the problem a certain kind of answer. *Will* never comes any time, but there has to be a will, and nothing pre-programs it.[11]

On the contrary, ratchet thinking interprets history as a mechanism that permits motion in one direction only. This is a progressivist constant: once a specific phase has been reached in evolution, for instance the advent of democracy in the nineteenth century, the process cannot be reversed, in the same way as a ratchet holds the spring tight when a clock is wound up. At the beginning of the twentieth century, liberals who believed in the irreversible progression of universal prosperity and peace were puzzled by the descent into militarism and war. In the 1930s, they wondered how the democratic social contract could be rescinded by fascism.

Marx's progressivist streak did not lead him to analyse capitalism as if it would meet a structural impossibility. Perhaps this was because he shared the optimism of this time. Later, as the expected revolution was not on the horizon, capitalist maturation was rationalised as the bearer—and prime agent—of the inescapable revolution that the proletarians were failing to achieve on their own. The historical problem that only proletarian action can solve was posed as already solved by capitalist evolution.

"There is nothing which has corrupted the German working-class so much as the opinion that they were swimming with the tide." (Walter Benjamin)

"The scientific-determinist aspect of Marx's thought was precisely what made it vulnerable to 'ideologisation,' both during his own lifetime and even more so in the theoretical heritage he left to the workers movement." (Guy Debord)[12]

3.5: "I Bring You Good Tidings"[13]

TC-SIC is certainly not swimming against the tide. There is nothing some people would love to hear more than the scientific proof that the end is nigh and human liberation is soon.

Class was and remains a problem.

TC-SIC offers the solution.

Communist theory as we understand it states that by reducing people to mere labour-power for sale and universalising this condition (which slavery for instance did not do), capitalism puts proletarians in a negative position: the negation of human potential, and the possibility of revolutionary negation.

TC-SIC "de-dialecticises" the definition by turning possibility into necessity. Class is no longer perceived as a relation that has to be superseded by those involved in it: class is what locks people into assigned roles, especially as producers, therefore class community is negative. Fortunately, working-class identity is impossible in our epoch, consequently . . .

SIC-TC's outlook reassures in two ways: it guarantees a bright future and, what is even more convenient, it is liable to be interpreted in a wide variety of ways.[14] Whatever its initial founders had in mind, this theory of class allows to empty class of class content, and then to fill it with many a content, as we will see in the next section: by reducing class to one oppressive identity among others, the TC-SIC perspective resonates with *identity politics*.

§ 4: Crossover Identity Politics

In the critique of *worker identity*, when TC laid the stress on *worker*, others heard *identity*.

From the start, TC's purpose has been to demonstrate that in the present capitalist phase the worker has no other option but to act as a proletarian. However TC defines class, its vision of communisation derives from *class* analysis.

For the other theorists this new section deals with, class is no longer what structures society, only what revolution is up against, and communisation becomes part of a critical discourse that focuses (more or less, depending on the author) on identity.[15]

Not really what the first promoters of "communisation theory" expected, but not an illogical step either.

Once theory has *dissociated the proletarian from the worker*, the revolutionary subject is to be found outside work and outside the workplace. So where? In the two or three billion jobless people, and among categories where, though many of their members may work, they do not act as workers but are moved by other determinations like gender and race. These categories engage in nonclass collectives with no privileged relation to work or the workplace. *Identity* has become the word that best encapsulates these categories and determinations.

Class . . . well, let's face it, there's a problem with the couple of unwaged unwageable billions. In the past, workers were an inward-looking class but at least theory knew what to expect from them. Now class has been extended to encompass most human beings. The world's wage-less dispossessed are worthy of the (alas, old-fashioned) name "proletarians" (as opposed to work-centred *workers*), but this vast mass is too remote, almost too powerful in its immensity to act as a quasi-universal proletarian *class* and pass as a credible substitute for the deceased working class.

In short, nothing seems to give consistency to "class" as the bearer of historical change.[16]

So the option is to come to terms, theoretically and politically, with *identity* politics: gender + class + race + sexuality ... The list is nonlimitative, and the words should be arranged in a circle, as in a round-robin signature, to avoid setting priorities: of all multiple contradictions within capitalist societies, class is only one.

Consequently, the theoretical challenge becomes how to weld together class and nonclass identities. Since the main characteristic of capitalism is dispossession and exclusion, how can *outside* people access and destroy the heart of the system that has rejected them? This approach requires endlessly recomposing a cross-identity alliance. A magazine's special issue on gender will be followed by one on race.

It is natural that the university should be the focal point of this quest. Campuses are a privileged spot for the self-criticism modern democracy specialises in. Universities' prime purpose remains to train the young for their future jobs, and of course only a few courses and PhDs can take Max Stirner or the Situationists as subject-matter, but social contradictions have to be researched, and it does not do any harm for the elite to be given a veneer of subversion.

Critical lecturers are exactly where they think they should be. Workerists used to get up early to hand out leaflets at factory gates, and even got jobs on the assembly line to be at the heart of things. Those who believe that struggles over reproduction are supplanting those over production logically want to act at the very core of reproductive processes.

What a university lecturer does best is construct, and a critical one deconstructs.

What do they de- or reconstruct?

In chapter 2, we saw how the notion of communisation reacted against a number of late twentieth-century attitudes, postmodernism being one of them. Now there is more postmodernism in current communisation discourse than meets the eye. The rejection of class analysis is linked with postmodern negation of universals: there is no such thing as a self, every identity is a construct, subjects are products of where they are situated. Anything that can be considered as *essentialist* is to be rejected. "Old" capitalism was founded on fixed identities, it had a centre, an essence which determined its series of identities: worker identity among others, also the father figure. In "new" capitalism, a subject only exists via a multiplicity of forms of experience: discourse, of course, power as well, because power is language and language is power. The world is not made of people: the world is made of stories. Society—at least modern society—is a self-driven circulating process without a focal causal point.

Applied to social analysis, this implies that there can be no single historical subject, only a heterogeneous flow of overlapping groups (workers, women, LGBTQ people, migrants, Native Americans, black people) organised in intersecting collectives, social centres, NGOs, info-kiosks . . . Class is considered divisive and dismissive: the true agent of change will be inclusive and take into account all forms of oppression, since all forms are prior to—or derivative of—one another.

What about social divides?

Suppose the discriminated-against black person is a business lawyer, and the oppressed woman owns a big store, how do they associate with an unemployed black woman? It seems to me that though the latter is clearly part of the revolutionary subject, the former two are unlikely partners for her, at least in the early days. A revolutionary subject can only be made of the oppressed and dispossessed of every category. Then why not speak of a . . . *proletariat*? Because this is precisely what post-class theory refuses: it wants a multilayered subject. Identity politics is Marxism gone multiculturalist.

In the real world, nothing shows that the reunion of the "outs" of the economy with those discriminated against on the basis of ethnicity, age, or sexual orientation, and with the largest cross-sectional category (women) will achieve what the industrial core has proved incapable of. Assuming the worker acting on the basis of his work *only* cared to improve his lot as a worker, why would groups acting on the basis of their respective categories do more than defend a combination of separate issues? There is less universality potential in (even intercon-nected) identities than in "class" as defined by communist theory (not by sociology). Faced with the worker/proletarian riddle, many Marxists have attempted to solve it on paper, and Théorie Communiste may not be the last to come up with the ultimate solution. More up-to-date theorists have years ahead of them to fine-tune class and identity concepts and leave rich pickings for commentators.

Meanwhile, whether identity groups are too heteroge-neous to converge or not, *communisation* provides common ground as an ideology of overall economic, societal, political and ecological change that is allegedly already happening—or on its way. (In that sense, it is part of the "communist ideol-ogy" mentioned in chapter 5, § 3.) Most readers of Marx still read him as the prophet of the working class taking over the world. Most readers of "communisation theory" read it as the demonstration of capitalism's final stage and of the immediacy of communism. Then *communisation* becomes what you put in it, depending on your personality and profession: one person will interpret it as an invitation to theoretical abstraction, another one to activism, a third one to artistic creation, the ideal being to combine all three: to expound in the morning, march in the afternoon and perform at night.

We should not be surprised that innocuous communi-sation has become fashionable. Debord's lionisation was a sign of things to come. At the beginning of the twenty-first century, a French magazine had quite a good special issue on Debord, with just one element missing: Debord's revolution-ary stand.[17] The common superficial reading of the SI indeed paved the way for another "recuperation," that of communisa-tion. Reducing the concept of *spectacle* to a denunciation of unreality and nonauthenticity contributed to installing the mental mapping that emphasises the *immateriality* of history, hence the inconsistency of identities, therefore of class reali-ties. That said, discourse never *completely* does away with *class*: it keeps it as an intellectual marker, a signpost that points to "radicalism."

What could be read in a literary monthly ten or twenty years ago is now taught at the university on both sides of the Atlantic. A lot of what is being said and written on "communisation" is relevant, only revolution is lacking, or what is called revolution is a nonrevolutionary revolution. A long time ago, the same happened to Marx, but the author of *Das Kapital* mostly wrote about class struggle, which is not enough today, so daily life and art (non-art art) have got to be added. A postmodern lecturer will teach poetics, political economy, and crisis. An essay will amalgamate Maoist philosopher Alain Badiou, Toni Negri, *Théorie Communiste*, and worker councilist Paul Mattick, and it does not matter if they are incompatible because, in the age of discontinued fragmentation, incongruities complement one another, and any reference is welcome, even "insurrection," as long as it is neutered by a merger with harmless terms. Like inviting a punk to a bourgeois party: turning revolt into style.

§ 5: The Proletariat as a Contradiction

Between the time when communisation started to be explicitly put forward and now, a considerable ideological shift has taken place.

As a concept, communisation was born out of the 1970s crisis where it never had even the limited influence of anti-bureaucratic or pro-council tendencies. It has now barely been fuelled by the new crisis: instead of clarifying the mental picture, current events breed confusion, because in reality there is little sign of a coming communising rupture.

As Magazine used to sing in 1978, communisation finds itself *shot by both sides*.

On one side, it is mixed with practices and attitudes entirely compatible with this society. In old (and not as dead as is often believed) reformism, union and party had a privileged role as intermediaries between militant labour and big business backed by the State. New daily life reformism dispenses with such mediators and relies on an informal network of practical and intellectual supporters who facilitate and theorise horizontalism, connectedness, cooperation, and sharing of what now exists. Popularised watered-down "communisation" fits in with what the "theory of the commons" keeps repeating: *common* wealth is there, all we have to do is reclaim it together.[18]

On the other side, there is a tendency to turn communisation into the theory-to-end-all-theories, with far less interest in communisation as a concrete transformation process, than as a means to define an entirely new epoch, when revolution is considered at last to be on the agenda. As if it was imperative and now possible to prove how "capitalist production begets, with the inexorability of a law of Nature, its own negation." (*Capital*, Vol. 1, chap. 32) This is wrong and—worse—pointless: communisation is an indispensable *concept*, not a *theory* to reinterpret and supersede the whole of past revolutionary thinking.

There's little chance that a man or woman who's never once felt the urge to blow something up will write meaningful subversive stuff. But the same is true of somebody who has never felt the derision of bookshelves full of revolutionary books and box files, or of the infinite availability of similar texts and archives on the internet.

A relevant theory is aware of its limits.

The activist pictures himself as a precipitant of events, and the grand theorist as the master of universal understanding. Both are drifters in the eye of the storm.

"I'd rather, once and for all, assign a distant future to revolution than have it forecast every day by *professional* revolutionaries that are proved wrong every day."[19]

In each period, communist theory expresses two things: the highest level reached by the previous insurrectionary phase; and the elements in contemporary proletarian struggles which seem to herald the content of new insurrections to come. The *incompleteness* of communist theory reflects the in-between-two-world situation of the proletarians, today's struggles no exception.

It is inevitable and necessary for revolutionaries to experience their time as the most favourable to revolution. This becomes absurd when one pictures oneself at the top of a privileged vantage point where it is possible to encompass the whole past and future, and to reveal the full meaning of human evolution.

However essential it is, the concept of communisation does not provide us with the ultimate answer to the revolutionary enigma, nor does it, once and for all, cut off an inevitably reformist past from a necessarily communist-prone present. We may be breaking new ground, but we are as time-bound today as Marx was in 1867 . . . or as we were in 1967.

Communisation will be possible because those who make the world can also unmake it, because the class of labour (whether its members are currently employed or out of a job) is also the class of the critique of work.

Marxists often turn this into formulaic dialectics, and non-Marxists make fun of it. Anyone who takes this definition seriously cannot evade the obvious: this duality is *contradictory*.

We have no other terrain apart from this inner conflict. It dramatically exploded in January 1919, when a few thousand Spartakist insurgents went to battle amid the quasi-indifference of nearly one million Berlin workers. Communisation will be the positive resolution of the contradiction, when the proletarians are able and willing to solve the social crisis by superseding capitalism. Therefore communisation will also be a settling of scores of the proletarian with herself and himself.

Until then, and as a contribution to this resolution, communist theory has to acknowledge the contradiction, and proletarians to address it.

■ NOTES

Communisation and My Discontent

1. Bruno Astarian, "Crisis Activity and Communisation," 2010, http://www.hicsalta-communisation.com/english/crisis-activity-and-communisation.

2. Benjamin Noys, ed., *Communization and Its Discontents: Contestation, Critique, and Contemporary Struggles* (New York: Autonomedia, 2011).

3. Outside the communisers' milieu, the communisation issue is further complicated by the popularity of the *commons* theory, according to which social change could come from collective usage and extension of what this theory presents as potentially common: for instance, communal or cooperative agricultural practices (where they still exist despite private property and globalisation) and free software access in the most modern countries. In other words, "creative commons" are supposed to allow a gradual and peaceful passage toward a human community. See chap. 7, note 18.

Chapter 1: Legacy

1. On democracy, see Gilles Dauvé, "Contribution to the Critique of Political Autonomy," libcom, 2008, https://libcom.org/library/implosion-point-democratist-ideology. Also: *The Implosion Point of Democratist Ideology*, from *Le Brise-Glace*, no. 2–3, Spring 1989, available at http://www.oocities.org/~johngray/impltitl.htm.

2. This description does not take into account the huge labour movement developing in Asia. And what about Latin America and Africa? The present analysis deals with what was until recently the driving force of world capitalism, and also the proletarian struggles' centre of gravity: the old industrial heartland, Western Europe, the United States, and Japan. The hub of power and movement upon which history depends may now be shifting to Asia. However, from the point of view of a "global" proletariat, there are as many commonalities as differences between present labour experience in China or India and what European workers went through in the early decades of industrialisation. We will go back to it in chapter 5.

3. *Capital*, vol. I, chap. 24, 3: "Accumulate, accumulate! That is Moses and the prophets! . . . Accumulation for accumulation's sake, production for production's sake: by this formula classical economy expressed the historical mission of the bourgeoisie."

4. Luc Boltanski and Eve Chiapello, *The New Spirit of Capitalism* (New York: Verso, 2007).

5.   *Invariance* started in 1968. A selection of Camatte's texts is available at the Marxists Internet Archive, https://www.marxists.org/archive/camatte/. For an example of the theory of a *consumer capitalism*, see the analyses of Bernard Stiegler.

6.   On SoB, see Marcel van der Linden, "Socialisme ou Barbarie: A French Revolutionary Group 1949–65," *Left History* 5, no . 1 (1997), http://www.left-dis.nl/uk/lindsob.htm. There is a biography of Fredy Perlman by his wife Lorraine: *Having Little, Being Much: A Chronicle of Fredy Perlman's Fifty Years* (Detroit: Black & Red, 1989). From the early 1960s until 1978, the *Groupe de Liaison pour l'Action des Travailleurs* (GLAT) published a well-researched theoretical bulletin.

7.   It may not be as banal as it seems. In the twenty-first century, debates on the "nature of the USSR" sound as dead as a dodo, and the ex-Stalinists have long ceased to be bogeymen. The French CP frequently rents out its headquarters to fashion designer shows and media events. With the demise of State capitalism, bureaucracy in general, and worker bureaucracy in particular, have left centre stage. This, however, is not the end of story. In anti-bureaucratic theory, the bureaucrats represented the new face and identity of the exploitative class that was replacing the bourgeoisie, but what mattered was the *perspective* derived from this: worker management, self-organisation, autonomy in the running of struggles. In the *worker bureaucracy v. worker democracy* confrontation, it was the last word that was essential and, in the requirement of worker democracy, democracy came first: not parliamentary democracy of course, but grassroots action, all power to the general assembly, collective decision-making, etc. When present-day councilists talk more of autonomous struggle than of worker democracy, it is because the latter includes the former. Also, there is much less space for anti-bureaucratic discourse since party and union bureaucracies have declined as institutions, so the critique has been expanded to target more porous and subtle means of imposing rules and norms upon us, in other words forms of *domination*.

8.   *Notes pour une analyse de la Révolution russe* was published in the Spring of 1968 under what was then my pen name, "Jean Barrot." It had no influence on the events and was only a little known later.

9.   On Censier, see Fredy Perlman, and Roger Grégoire, *Worker-Student Action Committees. France May 68*, 1969, https://libcom.org/library/worker-student-action-committees-france-1968-perlman-gregoire.

10. Miguel Amoros, "Report on the Assembly Movement," libcom, 1984, https://libcom.org/history/report-assembly-movement-miguel-amoros.

11. ICO's own analysis of '68, *La Grève généralisée. Mai–juin 1968*, does not seem to be available in English. ICO now exists as Echanges et mouvements (mondialisme.org). The Situationist critique of ICO is in the *SI* 11, 1967.

12. François Martin, "The Class Struggle and Its Most Characteristic Aspects in Recent Years," 1972, in *Eclipse and Re-emergence of the Communist Movement* (Oakland: PM Press, 2015), 67–89.

13. "Critique of Ultra-leftist Ideology" in *Eclipse and Re-emergence of the Communist Movement*.

Chapter 2: Birth of a Notion

1.   Harold Isaacs, *The Tragedy of the Chinese Revolution* (London: Secker and Warburg, 1938; revised ed. 1951), chap. 4.

2.   Jean-François Lyotard is now world-famous as a founding father of postmodernism for his *Postmodern Condition: A Report on Knowledge* (1979). It is interesting that his thesis was shored up less with social than with technological factors such as progress in communication, mass media, computers, and artificial intelligence. He then went on to theorise immateriality. We prefer to remember him for his 1956–63 articles on Algeria originally published in *Socialisme ou Barbarie* and collected in *La guerre des Algériens* (Paris: Galilee, 1989).

3.   An antidote to anti–working class talk and the myth of the classless society is Owen Jones, *Chavs: The Demonization of the Working Class* (New York: Verso, 2011).

4.   This theory has been developed in detail by *Temps Critiques* (tempscritiques. free.fr). Nothing is available in English as far as we know.

5.   *A Contribution to the Critique of Hegel's Philosophy of Right*, introduction.

6.   The brief survey above has left out the anti-industrial current because, unlike the others mentioned, class is not part of its starting point.

7.   Friedrich Engels, *The Part Played by Labour in the Transition from Ape to Man*, 1876.

8.   "With the seizing of the means of production by society, production of commodities is done away with, and, simultaneously, the mastery of the product over the producer. Anarchy in social production is replaced by systematic, definite organisation. . . . The whole mechanism of the capitalist mode of production breaks down under the pressure of the productive forces, its own creations. . . . The proletariat seizes political power and turns the means of production in the first instance into state property. But, in doing this, it abolishes itself as proletariat, abolishes all class distinctions and class antagonisms, abolishes also the state as state." (Engels, *Anti-Dühring*, 1877, part III, chap.2)

9.   After it was written in 1880, Paul Lafargue's *The Right to Be Lazy* became a classic in France among reformists as well as radicals. Much of its appeal was due to its being interpreted as the project of taking the best from capitalism (producing abundant goods) and doing away with the worst (exploiting the producers). According to it, the working day would be reduced to three hours, thanks to the "redeemer of mankind": the machine. Aristotle is famous for justifying slavery by the necessity that some people take care of basic needs to enable a minority to enjoy higher pursuits: "If . . . the shuttle would weave . . . , chief workmen would not want servants, nor masters slaves." Lafargue took the Greek philosopher at his word and declared that day had come. Social democrats and later Stalinists had no problem "recuperating" *The Right to Be Lazy*: for them, socialism was a decisive step forward of an industrial development which had hitherto only benefited the bourgeois but would be reoriented in the interest of the masses. In spite of its intuitive polemical vigour, Lafargue's attack on "the right to work" is a critique of neither wage-labour (selling and buying of human activity) nor work as separation (earning one's life before consuming thanks to the money earned).

10. According to his friend E. Delahaye, Rimbaud wrote in 1871 a *Project for a Communist Constitution*: direct democracy with delegates subject to frequent recall, a federation of communes, no money, compulsory work decided upon in common. Though Rimbaud took no part in the Paris Commune and almost certainly never read Marx, this is close to the communards' programme and the "associated producers" scheme.

11. As the councilist 1930s project has been considered in *Eclipse and Re-emergence of the Communist Movement* (Oakland: PM Press, 2015), it will not be examined here again.

12. Otto Rühle, *La crise mondial ou vers le capitalisme d'État*, published under the name of "Carl Steuerman" (Paris: Gallimard, 1932); no English edition is available.

13. For a critique of democracy, see Gilles Dauvé "Contribution to the Critique of Political Autonomy," libcom, 2008, https://libcom.org/library/a-contribution-critique-political-autonomy-gilles-dauve-2008.

14. On the history of the post-1917 Communist Left, see Denis Authier and Gilles Dauvé, "The Communist Left in Germany 1918–1921," originally published in French as "La Gauche Communiste en Allemagne (1918–1921)," English translation, 2006, https://www.marxists.org/subject/germany-1918-23/dauve-authier/index.htm.

    On the German Left, the Italian Left, the Socialisme ou Barbarie group, and the Situationist International, see the article "Recollecting Our Past," *La Banquise*, no. 2, 1983, https://libcom.org/files/Banquse_recollecting.pdf.

15. Few texts by Bordiga have been translated into English. A collection of ecological essays is titled *Murdering the Dead: Amadeo Bordiga on Capitalism and Other Disasters* (London: Antagonism Press, 2001), also available on libcom. To get an idea of his contribution, we could compare him to another prolific writer, the American Marxist Hal Draper, whose four-volume *Karl Marx's Theory of Revolution*, published from 1977 to 1990, is a very useful source of information. Draper gives a good compendium, and Bordiga contributed to a breakthrough.

16. Nikolai Bukharin, "The Economics of the Transition Period," 1920. In *The Politics and Economics of the Transition Period* (London: Routledge, 1979).

17. "The Communist Manifesto had, as its object, the proclamation of the inevitable impending dissolution of modern bourgeois property. But in Russia we find, face-to-face with the rapidly flowering capitalist swindle and bourgeois property, just beginning to develop, more than half the land owned in common by the peasants. Now the question is: can the Russian *obshchina*, though greatly undermined, yet a form of primeval common ownership of land, pass directly to the higher form of Communist common ownership? Or, on the contrary, must it first pass through the same process of dissolution such as constitutes the historical evolution of the West? The only answer to that possible today is this: If the Russian Revolution becomes the signal for a proletarian revolution in the West, so that both complement each other, the present Russian common ownership of land may serve as the starting point for a communist development." (Marx and Engels, preface to the 1882 Russian edition of the *Communist Manifesto*)

    On the *mir* and Russian populism, see Frano Venturi's excellent book, *Roots of Revolution: A History of the Populist and Socialist Movement in 19th Century Russia*, first published in 1952.

18. For example, Robert Service, *Trotsky: A Biography* (London: Macmillan, 2009), 282. This was the *Webster's* dictionary definition in 1961 and 1993, and roughly the one given by Wikipedia in 2010. Communists occasionally used *communisation* to mean effective takeover of power and the means of production by the proletariat, as opposed to "ambiguous" (social democrat) *socialisation* (*Le Soviet* 1, March 1, 1920).

19. Whoever coined the word, the idea was being circulated at the time in the small milieu round the Paris bookshop La Vieille Taupe ("The Old Mole") between 1965 and 1972. Since the May '68 events, the bookseller, Pierre Guillaume, a former member of Socialisme ou Barbarie and Pouvoir Ouvrier who was also for a while close to Guy Debord, had been consistently putting forward the idea of revolution as a communising process. Blanc was the first to publicly emphasise its importance. See *Un Monde sans argent* ("A World without Money"), https://libcom.org/library/world-without-money-communism-les-amis-de-4-millions-de-jeunes-travailleurs.

On the history and later evolution of that milieu, see "Recollecting Our Past," https://libcom.org/library/re-collecting-our-past-la-banquise.

20. Bruno Astarian, "Crisis Activity and Communisation," 2010, http://www.hicsalta-communisation.com/english/crisis-activity-and-communisation.

Chapter 3: Work Undone

1. *À l'Origine* (Xavier Giannoli, 2009).

2. On Engels, see *The Part Played by Labour in the Transition from Ape to Man*, 1876; and *Origin of the Family, Private Property and the State*, 1884.

3. For example, in the hunters' societies studied by French anthropologist Alain Testard (1945–2013), the group that specialises in hunting has no right to consume the animals it has killed, and must circulate them in return for the product of other activities: "what belongs to *oneself* is not *for oneself* . . . what comes *from oneself* is not to be consumed *by oneself*" (*Le Communisme primitif*, 1985). The more one learns about these societies, the more thought-provoking they are, and the more we realise how little they can enlighten us on communism in the sense we use the word.

4. *The Soul of Man under Socialism*, 1891.

5. Since some communisers see a commonality between communisation and *value-form theory* or *WertKritik*, as developed particularly by Robert Kurz, Anselm Jappe, and Moishe Postone . . . , a few words might be useful on what communisation and this theory share, or rather do not share.

Value-form theory emphasises value, but in its own special way.

Value is perceived as completely autonomised, self-propelled, all-absorbing in its course. All realities—production, work, class, even capital itself as a sum of money invested by an entrepreneur hoping to earn more at the end of the business cycle—all these concepts lose their functional specificity and melt into a great whole dominated by abstract labour. How does the system work? On its own.

Value-form theory does not ignore labour, but treats labour power as a commodity among thousands of others. The fact that this commodity is different because it produces value is deemed irrelevant, or it might have been relevant in the nineteenth century, but in late capitalism production has lost its distinctive importance, and separating "productive" from "unproductive" labour is part of "Marxist ballast."

Where is value produced? Everywhere. All previous categories are incorporated and dissolved into one. Capital is value and value is capital, but value-form theorists prioritise value because it is the abstraction of everything, similar to a seventeenth-century definition of God: "an infinite sphere the centre of which is everywhere, and the circumference nowhere." The upshot is that theorising value dilutes value.

Who (re)produces the world and therefore can overthrow it? Everyone, since everyone is involved in value circulation-production. Exploitation and alienation are equivalent. The consultant and her secretary, the shopkeeper and his assistant, the headmaster and the pupil, the town councillor and the garbage collector, we are all alienated by value, so let's all act wherever we are: since the dominion of value is everywhere, it can be questioned everywhere. Consequently, if value is all-pervading, it is a monster, but a potentially inconsistent one: because it resides in every act and every one of us, if more and more of us engage in nonmercantile practices, value becomes vulnerable. What Shakespeare called the "most operant poison"—money—will cease to operate when many of us stop drinking it. This is not dissimilar from "commons theory" in its practical consequences and preferences. Here too, we arrive at the 99 percent notion. Safety in numbers. (On commons theory, see chap. 7, n.18.)

Value-form theory owes its apparent radicalism to the fact that its major concepts have an all-encompassing look: "form" gives the impression of comprehending all sorts of contents, "abstract labour" the certainty of explaining every possible manifestation of work. In short, the reader thinks he is led from surface phenomena to the depth and generality of things. In fact, as concepts overstretch, they are emptied of content. "Abstract labour" means no labour, the inessentiality of work. "Form" means a shapeless, content-devoid reality. Back to postmodern *immateriality*: the rub is, even the immaterial has its origin which determines its inner process. (A plausible definition of postmodernism would be a lack of interest in real processes.)

There is hardly any commonality between value-form theory and communisation, at least as this book wishes to expound it. Society cannot be understood by bringing everything down to an essential (be it value or anything else), if this essential is turned into a self-perpetuating motion. Value is a *function* (not the driving force) of social (i.e., class) relations. Therefore social change is *not* a noncentered process, and the capital/labour relation *not* a minor issue.

For an in-depth critique of value-form theory, see Bruno Astarian in *Everything Must Go! The Abolition of Value* (Berkeley: Little Black Cart Books, 2015), https://libcom.org/library/everything-must-go-abolition-value-bruno-astarian-gilles-dauv%C3%A9.

6. In *Homo Ludens* (1938), Johan Huizinga reversed the traditional definition of man by work (*Homo faber*). Play comes first, Huizinga says: it is free, separate from "normal" life, imposes its own order and involves no material interest or gain. *Homo Ludens* reinterprets all human evolution in the light of play, as some historians reconstruct it as a series of economic stages from the cavemen to the landing on the Moon.

7. Writers and political activists like Selma James or, from another perspective, Italian autonomists insist on reinserting domestic unpaid woman labour within the analysis of capitalist production, and they campaign for the State to pay for this type of work (and other types, paying students for studying, for example). Waging the unwaged, in other words. For a critique of the theory of "reproductive labor," see Gilles Dauvé, "Federici versus Marx," 2015, https://troploin.fr/node/85.

8. This chapter owes its essentials to Marx and at the same time differs from him. As a critique of Marx can be read in *Eclipse and Re-emergence of the Communist Movement* (Oakland, PM Press, 2015), chap. 5. I thought it best here to express my views *directly*, without reexamining Marx.

9. Whereas most socialists wanted more industrialisation (albeit one that would benefit the masses), William Morris wished to reconcile industry with "arts and crafts," which meant a qualitative change in the productive process . . . and in life. (Still, his perspective kept money as a useful tool.)

Chapter 4: Crisis of Civilisation

1. Marshall Sahlins suggested the existence of a *domestic* mode of production, based on a peasant household-centred economy, with little exchange and hardly any money. From a very different angle, materialist feminist Christine Delphy takes up Marx's concept and duplicates it. Domestic labour (performed within the family by unpaid women for the benefit of men) is theorised as specific enough to be the basis of a *domestic* or *patriarchal* mode of production, which according to Delphy coexists with the capitalist mode in capitalist societies.

2. On historical progress/regress, see: Detlev J.K. Peukert, *The Weimar Republic: The Crisis of Classical Modernity* (New York: Hill and Wang, 1992; German edition, 1987).

3. Conan Fisher, *The Rise of the Nazis*, 2002. For a good book on Hitler's Germany see: Adam Tooze, *Wages of Destruction: The Making and Breaking of the Nazi Economy* (London: Allen Lane, 2006. On the 1917–37 period, see Gilles Dauvé, "When Insurrections Die," 1979, libcom, https://libcom.org/library/when-insurrections-die.

4. Ernst Nolte's highly objectionable book *Der europäische Bürgerkrieg* (*The European Civil War 1917–45*, published in Germany in 1987) has not been translated into English. It received flak from a variety of historians.

5. Eric Hopkins, *The Rise and Decline of the English Working Class 1918–90: A Social History* (New York: St. Martin's, 1991).

6. James O'Connor, *The Fiscal Crisis of the State* (New York: St. Martin's, 1973).

7. There appear to be two trends among critics of capitalism in its neoliberal phase. One school of thought, by far the best known, insists on the predatory role of finance over the "real" economy. Another school, without denying the impact of finance capital, doubts the present reality of this real economy. Though we won't pretend to settle a difficult question in a few lines, that second tendency has the merit of questioning not so much the share of the profits appropriated by a tiny minority, but the materiality of these profits. According to writers like Gopal Balakrishnan (*Speculations on the Stationary State*, in *New Left Review* 59, 2009), technological and social development has been

considerable—above all, in labour control—but has "failed to release a productivity revolution that would reduce costs and free up income for an all-round expansion" (Balakrishnan).

8.   Paul Mattick, *Marx and Keynes: The Limits of the Mixed Economy* (Boston: Porter Sargent, 1969).

9.   Tim Mason, *Nazism, Fascism and the Working Class* (Cambridge: Cambridge University Press, 1995).

10. Jean-Luc Gréau, *L'Avenir du capitalisme*, 2005. He used to be an economic expert for the main French business confederation.

11. In Bhutan and abroad, critics have raised the point that Bhutanese society is far from the exotic heaven of peace and harmony that its elite claims to be ruling. Labour exploitation is fierce, traditions oppressive, and minorities discriminated against. Well, only the gullible thought Shangri-La was real. But even if Bhutan was a tolerant, non-sexist, worker-friendly place, or if Gross National Happiness had been invented, say, in Denmark or Iceland, GNH would still be as misleading as GDP.

12. For instance, as early as 1956, Günther Anders was writing on *The Obsolescence of the Human Species*.

13. Clive Hamilton, *Earthmasters: The Dawn of the Age of Climate Engineering* (New Haven, CT: Yale University Press, 2013).

14. Sismondi (1773–1842) was one of the first underconsumptionist theorists. Observing the early nineteenth-century economic crises in England, he thought competition led to excessive cost-cutting, which lowered wages and prevented the workers from buying what they produced. The remedy was to pay them more so they would have enough purchasing power.

15. Anton Pannekoek, "The Theory of the Collapse of Capitalism" (1934), *Capital and Class* 1, no. 3 (Spring 1977): 59–81.

Chapter 5: Trouble In Class

1.   *The Paradox of Reformism: A Call for Economic Blockades*, from the Solidarity Federation website.

2.   On U.S. labour history, see Jeremy Brecher, *Strike!*, updated and expanded edition, PM Press, 2014.

3.   In 2012, the Maruti Suzuki workers went on strike again and rioted in support of wage-claims and in protest against casual temp labour. The manager was killed, the plant partly set on fire.

4.   George Katsiaficas, *Asia's Unknown Uprisings*, vol. 1, *South Korean Social Movements in the 20th Century* (Oakland: PM Press, 2012); and vol. 2, *People Power in the Philippines, Burma, Tibet, China, Taiwan, Bangladesh, Nepal, Thailand and Indonesia, 1947–2009* (Oakland: PM Press, 2013).

5.   A quite different point of view on the Occupy Movement in the United States can be read in *Internationalist Perspective* 56, 2012, and in *Anarchy* 72/73, 2012.

6.   TPTG (Ta Paidia Tis Galarias, or, "The Children in the Gallery," a group from Greece), "The Ivory Tower of Theory: A Critique of Théorie Communiste and 'The Glass Floor,'" 2010, libcom, https://libcom.org/library/ivory-tower-theory-critique-theorie-communiste-glass-floor.

7.   Matthew B. Crawford illustrates this ideologisation in his otherwise stimulating *Shop Class as Soulcraft: An Inquiry into the Value of Work* (New

York: Penguin, 2009). Not often is a writer both a philosopher and a mechanic. The author's personal experience contributes to his debunking the myth of the all "knowledge" society where most jobs of the future would have us sit in front of a screen. His insistence on self-reliance is most welcome, "and it becomes possible once again to think the thought: Let me make myself useful. . . . We want to feel that the world is intelligible, so we can be responsible for it." This is a good antidote to the "computer revolution" illusion of mastering the world (and our lives), when in fact we are using machines we know next to nothing about.

A return to craftsmanship and local community, however, is now only possible on the margin of society. Motorbike repair shops are no match for the rule of big business. Where and how are motorbikes manufactured?

8. According to her biography by J.-P. Nettl (1966), in her articles, speeches, and daily activity, Rosa Luxemburg rarely referred to her thesis on the collapse of capitalism that she had expounded in *The Accumulation of Capital*.

Chapter 6: Creative Insurrection

1. On "anti-proletarian" practices, see Bruno Astarian, "Crisis Activity and Communisation," 2010, http://www.hicsalta-communisation.com/english/crisis-activity-and-communisation.

2. John H. Goldthorpe, *The Affluent Worker: Political Attitudes and Behaviour* (London: Cambridge University Press, 1968).

3. Prole.info, *Abolish Restaurants* (Oakland: PM Press, 2010), 8.

4. Astarian, "Crisis Activity and Communisation." For more on the sex/gender issue, see Gilles Dauvé, *On the "Woman Question"*, 2016: https://troploin.fr/node/88.

5. Popular revolts also rarely bother about people locked up in jails or lunatic asylums. Though masculine domination is far more central, the extent that insurgents do not demand an end to imprisonment and incarcerations of all types, is the extent to which their self-organisation is weak and still dominated by bourgeois concerns.

6. Mary Wollstonecraft wrote *A Vindication of the Rights of Woman* in 1792. Her husband William Godwin was one of the early anarchists (*Enquiry Concerning Political Justice*, 1793). Their daughter Mary (author of *Frankenstein*) married Percy Shelley, poet, radical, and supporter of workers' struggles. An interesting family. On the thorny and highly charged question of race and class, see Gilles Dauvé, *White Riot: Race & Class in 20th Century South Africa*, 2018: https://troploin.fr/node/93.

7. This is where sexism differs deeply from racism, which has more to do with "divide and conquer." Remembering that *race* is a historical notion: the United States debated in the early twentieth century about Finnish immigrants being "Mongol," that is, nonwhite.

8. In 1846, Marx's (unpublished) view was more accurate: "marriage, property, the family . . . are the practical basis on which the bourgeoisie has directed its domination. . . . One cannot speak at all of the family "as such." In the eighteenth century the concept of the [feudal] family was abolished by the philosophers, because the actual family was already

in the process of dissolution. . . . The internal family bond, the separate components constituting the concept of the family were dissolved, for example, obedience, piety, fidelity in marriage, etc.; but the real body of the family, the property relation, the exclusive attitude in relation to their families, forced cohabitation—relations determined by the existence of children, the structure of modern towns, the formation of capital, etc.—all these were preserved, along with numerous violations, because the existence of the family is made necessary by its connection with the mode of production. . . . The family continues to exist even in the nineteenth century, only the process of its dissolution has become more general . . . because of the higher development of industry and competition." (*German Ideology*, chap. 3, Miscellaneous, "The Family").

On the subject of Marx and the family, an interesting read is Mary Gabriel, *Love and Capital: Karl and Jenny Marx and the Birth of a Revolution* (New York: Little, Brown and Co., 2011).

On family and child/adult relation, see our *Alice in Monsterland*, in Anthony Leskov, *Communicating Vessels: An Anthology*, Communicating Vessels Books, 2006.

9. The family in North America and Europe is becoming more equal, with less unequal divisions of housework and childcare. There is an increasing acceptance of homosexuality in mainstream life. These facts do not break the link between private property, inheritance, and the family.

10. "Resistance Is Possible," 1984 interview with two members of Rote Zora, http://libcom.org/library/resistance-possible-excerpts-interview-two-anonymous-members-red-zora.

11. *Eclipse and Re-emergence of the Communist Movement* (Oakland: PM Press, 2015), chap. 1, § 11: "States and How to Get Rid of Them."

12. *We Are the 1%*, from Czech group Tridni Valka (Class War). In English on the finimondo.org site.

13. Community currencies and the "equal time, equal value" principle have their supporters and prophets. One is Paul Glover (*Hometown Money*, 2013).

14. Jane Bowles, *Two Serious Ladies*, 1943. She married composer and (later) writer Paul Bowles, author of *The Sheltering Sky*. One of those people with too much to say to be able to express it, she only wrote one novel, a play, and a few short stories. In 1957, she had a stroke and spent most of her remaining life in hospitals. See *My Sister's Hand in Mine: The Collected Works of Jane Bowles* (New York: Farrar, Straus and Giroux, 2005), and her biography by Millicent Dillon, *A Little Original Sin* (New York: Holt, Rinehart, and Winston, 1981).

Chapter 7: A Veritable Split

1. *Théorie Communiste* (founded in 1977 and based in France): https://sites. google.com/site/theoriecommuniste/home. *SIC* is an international discussion group born in 2009, some of its participants still active in the project, others not, new ones joining. *Théorie Communiste* left in 2013. Texts and related groups accessible at sicjournal.org. For a presentation of SIC's "common ground": sicjournal.org/about/.

2. See in particular his politics in 1848–49 as the editor of the bourgeois liberal *New Rheinland Gazette*, "Organ of Democracy." To get an idea of

Marx's political activity, a good way is to read his correspondence, and biographies like the one by Franz Mehring, *Karl Marx: The Story of His Life* (London: Routledge, 2010 [1918]).

3. Important anarchist thinkers like Kropotkin and Elisée Reclus (both renowned professional geographers) also supported deterministic views, with an emphasis more on social organisation than production. To them, the worldwide spread of industry and commerce created a potentially universal humane society where ethnic differences, borders, and States were made meaningless. In much of anarchist as well as Marxist thinking, society ceased to be seen as the result of relationships between beings and classes, and revolution was supposed to happen because of a universal drive toward a unified humankind.

4. In the real working world, there are at least as many work dodgers as work glorifiers, but this will be dismissed as superficial psychologising, so let's not be bothered.

5. Michael Seidman, *Workers against Work: Labor in Paris and Barcelona during the Popular Fronts* (Berkeley: University of California Press, 1991); "To Work or Not to Work? Is That the Question?," 2005, libcom, https://libcom.org/library/to-work-or-not-to-work-dauve.

6. *Revolutionary syndicalism* truly stood for a union-organised worker society. It dominated the French CGT (founded in 1895) until the beginning of the twentieth century. Then the confederation went the way unionism usually goes: a reformist one. In spite of its militancy, the Unione Sindicale Italiana (launched in 1912 and which comprised revolutionary syndicalists and anarchists) was never strong enough to threaten the hegemony of the socialist-led CGIL.

   A lot of the rank and file of the English Socialist Labour Party left the party and joined the newborn CPGB in 1920. The American Socialist Labor Party (founded in 1876) lost before 1914 what little influence it had. Both SLPs advocated *revolutionary* (or *socialist*) *industrial unionism*, on the lines of De Leon. If we leave the history of ideas aside, the practical effect of this working-class tendency was to contribute to unionism in the form of the industrial unionism of the later CIO.

   For the record, De Leon (1852–1914) disagreed with *syndicalism* because he thought a political party (and parliamentary action) was necessary. He had a difficult relation with the IWW who eventually expelled him. He believed a peaceful parliamentary socialist victory would help workers, miners, farmers, etc. formerly organised in industrial unions, to create worker councils which would seize the means of production. The elected government would give way to a democracy of worker councils, and from then on an All-Industrial Congress would act as the real government.

   Apart from Spain and the CNT, the only area where syndicalists kept strongholds in the working class after 1914–18 was Latin America, Argentina especially.

7. Australia is a case in point: it had the first socialist electoral majority and the first Labour government in 1905, which for decades supported *white only* organised labour as a closed-in community within capitalism and against foreign (Asian) workers.

8.   On the "us/them" worker self-awareness in England in the 1940s and
      '50s, Richard Hoggart, *The Uses of Literacy*, 1957.

9.   In the "unpublished sixth chapter of *Capital*" (part of his 1861–65 manu-
      scripts), Marx distinguishes between labour's *formal* submission, based
      on the lengthening of the work day and the extensive exploitation
      of labour, and *real* submission, based on shorter but more intensive
      working hours. That distinction does not separate two successive
      periods: formal and real submission combine. Capital's formal domina-
      tion is not a remnant that has to be disposed of for the system to fully
      mature, but a component of real domination. Subcontracting enables
      "modern" companies to stay profitable by having manufacturing done
      overseas where labour is cheap.

10.   If you ask why there are so few signs of a consistent communising
      current among proletarians, you will be told that proof of a "new cycle
      of struggles" is to be found in the negative: in our time, when the proles
      can't defend themselves against capital, it means they're about to attack
      it. They appear to do little because only frontal assault is now on the
      agenda. Presence demonstrated by absence. Weakness is strength.
      Defeat today proves victory tomorrow. Dialectics works wonders.

11.   Debate is impossible with people who cannot bear the use of words like
      choice, *desire*, or *will*, people who prefer to ground their allegedly rigorous
      vocabulary in a historically emotionless framework. People, in other
      words, who negate their own subjectivity. The trouble with refusing to
      acknowledge oneself as a subject with one's personal experience and
      feelings is that the repressed ego often bursts back in the form of self-
      satisfaction or competitiveness.

12.   Benjamin, *On the Concept of History*, 1940, § XI; Debord, *Society of the
      Spectacle*, 1967, thesis 84.

13.   Luke 2:10.

14.   This drift is illustrated by the disastrous substitution of *communisers* for
      "communists." Since SIC-TC claims to have found in communisation a
      whole new understanding of the capitalist and proletarian course, the
      inventors have been named after their discovery. Yet the choice of this
      word entails confusion. A *communist* supports and possibly fights for
      communism. A *communiser* is involved in communising, which only
      takes place in a revolutionary process, so at the time of writing, no one
      is a communiser. Confusion is all the more damaging as "commons
      theory" defenders speak as if "the common" was *already* being imple-
      mented (see note 18).

15.   This section refers to an elastic range of theories, from representatives
      of a "class + identity" mix like Endnotes, to such an ever-expanding
      panorama of writers that naming two or three would be unfair to others,
      and all are easily accessible in the cyber world. *Endnotes* (based in Britain
      and the United States): endnotes.org.uk.

16.   If the reader thinks I am going too far in my description of the drift
      toward a total *decoupling of the proletarian from work*, and then *of the revolu-
      tion from class*, here is a quote: "The notion of a 'contradiction between
      classes' appears to be of strictly Maoist lineage. Some have defended its
      Marxian imprimatur by pointing to a passage in the Penguin translation

of the *Grundrisse*, where Marx refers to a 'contradiction of capital and wage labour' ([MECW 29], 90, Nicholaus trans.). But the term here is *Gegensatz* (opposition), rather than *Widerspruch* (contradiction). We can find no reference in Marx's work to a contradiction between 'capital and labour', or 'capitalists and workers'." (*Endnotes* 3, 2013, "Editorial," § 3). I'm gegensatzed.

17. *Le Magazine Littéraire* 399, June 2001.

18. Confusion is common between communisation and commons theory. The latter is grounded on the idea that community, cooperation, and solidarity links as they now exist could develop into social dynamics strong enough to ultimately overthrow the domination of capital and State power. This applies to precapitalist village communal ties in the Nordeste as well as to hi-tech office work in New York: according to *commons* advocates, computer knowledge is collectively part of us, all we have to do is repossess what is already ours.

    The attraction of this theory has little to do with its feasibility. Few people believe that the revival of small communities will eradicate inequality in Brazil, that the internet and "creative commons" are the way to a nonmercantile chummy world, or that millions of co-ops will run multinationals out of business.

    The *commons theory* appeals because of its strong language ("subversion," "mass civil war against world capital" . . .) and above all because it promises more than a fair redistribution of wealth: it talks about how we *live* together, and promises a qualitative change that neither traditional reformers nor the declining welfare state are apt to deliver. See Hardt and Negri, *Commonwealth*, 2011.

    Whereas Negri and others situate the possibility of change in modern technology, David Graeber—a prominent "99 percent" theorist—sees it in anthropological data. Human sociability is founded upon what he calls "baseline communism": cooperation, personal interaction, reciprocity, grassroots democracy, sharing of tools and products, etc. An anarchist like Kropotkin might have embraced a similar vision of human nature, but for him, without revolution, this undercurrent would remain below the surface of history. Though David Graeber calls himself an *anarchist anthropologist*, he believes that change will come via the progressive emergence and expansion of communistic attitudes and practices into the whole of social life. Here again, gradualism is expressed in extreme wording. See the review of his *Debt: The First 5,000 Years* (2011), in *Wildcat* 93, Summer 2012.

19. *Hurrah!!! ou la Révolution par les Cosaques*, 1854, by Ernest Coeurderoy (1825–62), French revolutionary and anarchist, who had to live in exile after 1849, and killed himself in Switzerland.

■ ABOUT THE AUTHOR

Born in 1947, **Gilles Dauvé** has worked as a translator and a schoolteacher. He is the author of essays and books on the Russian, German, and Spanish revolutions, and on democracy, fascism, war, morals, crisis, and class. In English, his texts *What Is Situationism?* and *Fascism/Anti-Fascism* (both written under the pseudonym Jean Barrot) have led a legendary existence in the samizdat pamphlet underground. His collection of essays titled *Eclipse and Re-emergence of the Communist Movement* has been published in many editions, including an expanded edition in the PM Press Revolutionary Pocketbooks series. In 2015, he wrote "An A to Z of Communisation" in *Everything Must Go! The Abolition of Value*, a book coauthored with Bruno Astarian, published by Little Black Cart Books. It is also available online at https://troploin.fr/node/87.

ABOUT PM PRESS

PM Press was founded at the end of 2007 by a small collection of folks with decades of publishing, media, and organizing experience. PM Press co-conspirators have published and distributed hundreds of books, pamphlets, CDs, and DVDs. Members of PM have founded enduring book fairs, spearheaded victorious tenant organizing campaigns, and worked closely with bookstores, academic conferences, and even rock bands to deliver political and challenging ideas to all walks of life. We're old enough to know what we're doing and young enough to know what's at stake.

We create radical and stimulating fiction and non-fiction books, pamphlets, T-shirts, visual and audio materials to educate, entertain, and inspire you. We aim to distribute these through every available channel with every available technology—whether that means you are seeing anarchist classics at our bookfair stalls; reading our latest vegan cookbook at the café; downloading geeky fiction e-books; or digging new music and timely videos from our website.

PM Press is always on the lookout for talented and skilled volunteers, artists, activists, and writers to work with. If you have a great idea for a project or can contribute in some way, please get in touch.

PM Press
PO Box 23912
Oakland, CA 94623
www.pmpress.org

PM Press in Europe
europe@pmpress.org
www.pmpress.org.uk

FRIENDS OF PM PRESS

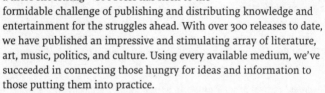

These are indisputably momentous times—the financial system is melting down globally and the Empire is stumbling. Now more than ever there is a vital need for radical ideas.

In the seven years since its founding—and on a mere shoestring—PM Press has risen to the formidable challenge of publishing and distributing knowledge and entertainment for the struggles ahead. With over 300 releases to date, we have published an impressive and stimulating array of literature, art, music, politics, and culture. Using every available medium, we've succeeded in connecting those hungry for ideas and information to those putting them into practice.

Friends of PM allows you to directly help impact, amplify, and revitalize the discourse and actions of radical writers, filmmakers, and artists. It provides us with a stable foundation from which we can build upon our early successes and provides a much-needed subsidy for the materials that can't necessarily pay their own way. You can help make that happen—and receive every new title automatically delivered to your door once a month—by joining as a Friend of PM Press. And, we'll throw in a free T-shirt when you sign up.

Here are your options:

- **$30 a month** Get all books and pamphlets plus 50% discount on all webstore purchases

- **$40 a month** Get all PM Press releases (including CDs and DVDs) plus 50% discount on all webstore purchases

- **$100 a month** Superstar—Everything plus PM merchandise, free downloads, and 50% discount on all webstore purchases

For those who can't afford $30 or more a month, we're introducing **Sustainer Rates** at $15, $10 and $5. Sustainers get a free PM Press T-shirt and a 50% discount on all purchases from our website.

Your Visa or Mastercard will be billed once a month, until you tell us to stop. Or until our efforts succeed in bringing the revolution around. Or the financial meltdown of Capital makes plastic redundant. Whichever comes first.